BEING A

BEING
A FATHER

FAMILY,
WORK,
AND SELF

MOTHERING MAGAZINE

Edited by Anne Pedersen and Peggy O'Mara

John Muir Publications
Santa Fe, New Mexico

John Muir Publications, P.O. Box 613, Santa Fe, NM 87504

© 1990 by Mothering Magazine
Cover © 1990 by John Muir Publications
All rights reserved. Published 1990
Printed in the United States of America

First edition. First printing

Library of Congress Cataloging-in-Publication Data

Being a father : family, work, and self / Mothering magazine; edited
  by Anne Pedersen and Peggy O'Mara. — 1st. ed.
    p. cm.
  Revised essays which originally appeared in Mothering magazine.
  ISBN 0-945465-69-6
    1. Fatherhood—United States. 2. Fathers—United States—
Psychology. I. Pedersen, Anne, 1949- . II. O'Mara, Peggy.
III. Mothering.
HQ756.B44 1990
306.874'2—dc20

90-33481
CIP

Distributed to the book trade by:
W. W. Norton & Company, Inc.
New York, New York

Cover illustration and overall design: Sally Blakemore
Typographer: Copygraphics, Inc.
Printer: McNaughton & Gunn, Inc.
Back Cover Photo: © Skjold Photography

Contents

FOREWORD

It has taken me twenty-three years of parenting seven children to learn how to be a father. In fact, I am still learning; my children haven't finished with me yet.

When my wife's and my first two children were small, I was neither a very involved dad nor a supportive husband. In retrospect, I realize that I married before I was really mature. I was a boy, not yet ready to think like a man. Our first two children—beautiful sons—came at a time when I was climbing the ladder of professional success. I embraced wholeheartedly a system of medical training that preached profession first and left family a distant second. It is ironic that I chose to work at a profession dedicated to helping families thrive but that my own family barely survived the rigors of my early years as a doctor. My wife, Martha, told me later, "I suspected we were in for trouble when you took a suitcase full of medical books along on our honeymoon."

A pediatrician should know better, right? Well, I didn't. I was not deliberately an absentee father, but I did feel that my first responsibility was to establish my career, from which my family would ultimately profit. Also, I didn't think that a father's role was all that important in the first few years of life. A mother's care seemed to be enough for young children. My father had been only minimally involved in our family when I was growing up, and somehow I managed to tune out any realization of the importance of a father's presence.

By the time we were pregnant with our sixth child, Matthew (who at that time we thought would probably be our last), things had changed. Now I wanted to be a very involved father and become very close to our new child. My wife had often described her relationship to our babies by saying that she felt "absolutely addicted" to them. I wanted to feel "addicted," too. After all, half of those forty-six chromosomes in every cell of our children came from me.

Is it possible for a father to be as close to a baby as a mother? The baby comes out of the mother's body, so it seems natural that there

would be a stronger mother-child bond than father-child bond.
While I was prepared to accept whatever scientific facts explained the
mother-baby relationship, I wondered if there was an additional
explanation for this "addiction" my wife spoke of. Perhaps such bonding was a by-product of simply spending more time with the baby?
Whatever it was that provided the magical glue cementing mother
and baby together, I wanted some of it. Although I realized I could
not manufacture for myself the hormones that travel through a
mother's internal highways and tell her which turns to take, nor
could I breast-feed the baby, I was determined to become a 100 percent father—the best darn father in the whole wide world! Mindful of
the familiar commercial slogan, "Be all that you can be," I knew that I
wanted to be all that I could be as a father.

Shortly before Matthew's birth, I moved my medical practice into
our home, renovating an area in our garage into a medical office. The
children called this "Dr. Bill's garage." I was not only present at
Matthew's birth but also intimately involved. Rather than acting as
"labor coach," calling out all the signals that we had learned in childbirth class, I embraced and loved my wife during our labor, a role that
came more naturally. I feel that men should coach sports, not laboring
women. It is much better to hire a female labor support person to do
the "coaching" and allow a father to perform his husbandly role, in
which he is usually more comfortable.

I was the first person to touch our baby. As his slippery little body
slid into my anxious hands, I knew that we were destined for a special
relationship. He breathed immediately; so did I. Martha instinctively
reached down and gently pulled Matthew up to her breast. As I cut
the umbilical cord, I felt that I was giving Matthew and Martha permission to momentarily separate and then quickly reunite, continuing
their feeling of oneness in a different way.

During his first month, Matt always seemed to be in skin-to-skin
contact with one of his parents, usually his mom but quite often me.
After Martha nursed him, I would frequently say to her, "Now it is my
turn." She would drape our limp and satisfied baby over my bare
chest, and we would drift off to sleep together. I could sense that Matt
knew that my body was different from his mom's; he nestled under my
chin as if trying to find a warm corner in this new "womb."

My son and I spent a lot of time together: we were buddies from
birth. I began to feel what Martha meant when she said she felt

addicted to our babies. I felt right when Matthew and I were together and not right when we were apart. Contrary to my previous history, I shortened my office hours during the first month of his life and tried to be with him as much as possible. When I was with him, I was totally there—physically and mentally.

But I also realized that the ideal of full-time fatherhood was seldom achievable. I was plagued by that four-letter word, w-o-r-k. Initially, I was a bit envious that I couldn't sit home all day and just enjoy the luxury of holding and nurturing Matthew. But I realized that I wasn't really designed to do that. Still, more than biology was at fault here. Our society has traditionally ignored the emotional needs of new fathers. At the very least, there ought to be a law granting new dads paternity leave.

After a few months, I was addicted to Matt, just as I had wanted to be, but it was a different level of addiction than Martha's. Matt and I had a different relationship than Martha and Matt. Not better, not worse, just different. She was close to him, I was close to him, but we were close to him in different ways. Matthew didn't love me more or less than Martha; he loved me differently. I guess part of the reason for this was that we gave differently to Matt, so he gave differently in return to each of us. Martha really gave Matthew part of herself—her milk. My giving seemed more indirect at times. I gave to Matt by giving to Martha. I also gave to the rest of the family what they were used to getting from Martha, so she had more to give to Matt. I could not breast-feed Matthew, but I could create a supportive environment, which made it easier for Martha.

After a few months of my newly involved fathering, rewards began to come my way. I found that I could nurse Matthew, nursing in this case meaning complete nurturing and not just breast-feeding. I refused diplomatically to be labeled as a substitute mother. I was not just pinch-hitting for Martha, the "real" nurturer; I had my own unique way of nurturing Matthew—not better than Martha's, not worse, just different.

There were two uniquely male nurturing styles that Matthew liked best. One was the "warm fuzzy," when he would drape his bare chest over mine, placing his ear over my heartbeat, and we would drift off to sleep together. The other was the "neck nestle," in which I placed Matthew's head against my throat and draped my chin over his head. In the neck nestle, fathers have a slight edge over mothers. Babies hear not only through their ears but also through the vibration of their skull bones. When a father places his baby's skull against his voice box and hums or sings, the slower, more easily felt vibrations of the lower-pitched male voice often lull the baby right to sleep. An added attraction of the neck nestle is that the baby feels the warm air from his father's nose on his scalp. Experienced mothers have long known that sometimes just breathing onto their babies' faces or heads will calm them. They call this "magic breath."

Fathering is not all giving-giving-giving. True, in the early years babies are primarily takers and fathers primarily givers, but even in those first few months Matthew gave something back to me. Because I was around and involved, he responded to my nurturing in a way that made me feel on top of the world. This newly discovered, involved fathering also taught me sensitivity. His cries bothered me more and stimulated me to develop uniquely male ways of dealing with baby distress. The neck nestle usually worked the best.

My new nurturing abilities and sensitivity carried over into our marriage. Martha had no trouble releasing Matthew into my care, because from the moment of birth I had proven my capabilities. New dads, a word of advice: when you do not become available and involved in the care of your tiny infant, your wife will take up the slack and become very attached to the baby. Moreover, an uninvolved or absent father is at risk for developing male postpartum depression—that left-out feeling that occurs when a father has not taken the opportunity to develop the nurturing skills necessary to help his wife and comfort his baby. When, after months of practice, my nurturing skills developed, I found that not only was I becoming more sensitive to Matthew but I was also becoming more sensitive to Martha as well. She, in turn, became more sensitive to me. This mutual sensitivity greatly improved our marriage and our sexuality. Nothing turns a woman on more than the support of a caring and nurturing husband.

Matthew is now four and a half years old. Since this experiment in "attachment fathering" began, we have grown very close, and he has taught me how richly rewarding this involved style of fathering can be. My only regret is that it took me six children to discover this. I have vowed to strike a balance between being, first, a committed father and, second, a practicing physician, teacher, and lecturer to parent groups. When outside commitments pile up, I feel stretched, but my commitment to achieve proper balance acts like a strong rubber band, pulling me back to Matthew and the rest of the family. The rubber band does not break. I don't let it get stretched that far. The older children in our large family have also profited from witnessing my growth as a nurturing father. Both the girls and the boys have learned healthy sexual role models by observing how I treat their little brother and their mother. Becoming a nurturing father is indeed a long-term investment.

The older Matthew gets and the more we both grow in our relationship, the more I am realizing the payoff of those early years of nurturing. As a child grows older, a father's major role is often that of disciplinarian and guiding authority figure to the child. Why has it been so much easier than with my other children for me to discipline Matthew and for Matthew to receive my discipline? The answer is that I became a sensitive nurturer of Matthew first and then later his effective authority figure. How unwise it is for a father to suddenly become involved and begin delivering heavy-handed discipline when a child is old enough to, say, throw a football. This type of discipline doesn't work, because there exists no foundation of trust or respect of the child toward the father, as the father did not develop the nurturing skills necessary to build that trust.

Being a Father: Family, Work, and Self addresses beautifully the conflicts and joys of today's concerned fathers. I am amazed at how quickly and how much the fathers who share their experiences in this book have learned—in a much shorter time than it took me. This book drives home the value of fatherhood. Many of today's fathers must become more involved in their children's lives out of necessity, if not out of desire. If mothers are required to share more of the task of generating family income, fathers will be forced to share more of the child care. *Being a Father* shows new dads how. Nothing matures a man more than nurturing his children. The advice shared by the fathers in this book will add a bit of maturity to us all.

—William Sears

PART I:
BECOMING A FATHER

PREGNANT FATHERS

Jack R. Heinowitz

"Father: One who begets or has begotten a child ."
—Webster's Third New International Dictionary

M ost of us would probably agree that Webster's definition of a "father" hardly begins to encompass the broad range of images, feelings, and reactions the word conveys today. As our ideas about sex roles have loosened and our concept of family has broadened, more and more fathers are questioning the value and desirability of taking on the traditional fathering roles they learned growing up in their own families.

I have had the good fortune and pleasure to meet and work with a growing number of men who are in the process of reassessing their personal values and priorities. Many have realized that imitating the father-as-provider image they grew up with does not satisfy deeper needs for self-expression, creativity, and personal growth or for closer, more meaningful contact with their children, partners, and friends.

My relationships with my daughter Becky, now fifteen, and my stepdaughter, Eden, have been among the most challenging and gratifying ventures of my life. However, they certainly haven't been easy. Becoming the kind of father I want to be has meant looking back, reliving, and analyzing many of my childhood experiences (pleasant and unpleasant); examining the attitudes and values I've learned about being a man, a father, and a partner; *un*learning much of what I've been taught and practicing the lessons I do value; continually redefining my sense of purpose and my ideas about masculinity and relationships; and saying good-bye to my old relationship with my parents while simultaneously establishing a new, more equal "parent-to-parent" relationship with them as well as with my wife.

Today's Fathers
Today's fathers face dramatically new and changing expectations as parents. They are expected to become actively involved in pregnancy,

childbirth, child care, and household chores; to be nurturing, sensitive, and expressive; and to fulfill their customary work responsibilities as well. Today's fathers may well be facing the economic and psychological realities of a two-career family: inflation; being a stepparent, a custodial, or noncustodial parent; as well as geographic separation from their families and communities of origin. In short, today's fathers are being asked to fulfill roles that more often than not they have never experienced themselves and for which they are not likely to be prepared. Quite a task, indeed!

It is no wonder, then, that many new fathers approach fatherhood with a mixture of feelings, including uncertainty and apprehension as well as enthusiasm and optimism. Only very recently have we begun to regard parenting as a joint venture, shared by mothers and fathers. Traditionally, mothers have been presumed to be the more "natural" and "more qualified" parents. We have attributed "mothering instincts" to women (and to some tender men) but have never developed the concept of "fathering instincts." For too long and for too many, fathering has meant sacrificing the pleasures of participating in daily family life and close family relationships in favor of seeking personal satisfaction and external rewards through business success, wealth, and professional recognition.

The crippling effect this social conditioning can and does have on some aspiring fathers can be profound. As one expectant father confided: "I don't feel as strongly for my father as I do my mother. I think that's bound up in the fact that mothers and children have very strong feelings for each other—something qualitatively different from what a man can have with his child. I want to be as close to my child as my wife is, but can I really?"

The Importance of Fathers

A common misconception in our culture is that fathers have little effect on their children's development, particularly during the first year of life. As a result, many fathers stand back and wait to bond with their children until they are older, thus missing out on rich and varied opportunities to establish a unique and special relationship with their infants.

In fact, infants feel no innate preference for one parent over the other. They respond to being held, touched, stimulated, and gratified

as well as to being breast-fed. Being emotionally present and respon-
sive to your child is clearly more important than the amount of time
you spend together or even what you do during that time. Studies
of children deprived of close father contact have shown repeatedly
that these children have greater difficulty developing self-esteem,
adjusting socially and sexually, and coping with frustration than children with involved fathers.

Fathers, Sons, and Daughters
For a young boy, quality time with dad—his primary male model
throughout life—confirms his sense of worthiness, competence, and
masculinity. For a daughter, time with dad provides her first relationship with someone of the opposite sex. Her impressions of her father
and the lessons she learns from watching and being with him will
color and shape her perceptions of herself as a female, of men as partners and fathers, and of male-female relationships in general. A
father's attention, care, and positive interaction convey deeply felt
and essential messages of acceptance, approval, and appreciation to
his daughter. For both sons and daughters, their father's relationship
with their mother will significantly influence ideas and expectations
about love, sharing, cooperation, tolerance, solving problems, and
handling differences.

A Father's Dilemma
Unfortunately, a man's insecurity about his ability to bond with and
relate meaningfully to his developing child is often unintentionally
reinforced during pregnancy, as he experiences friends' and relatives'
attention and interest turning primarily to his pregnant partner.
His transition to fatherhood is not acknowledged, supported, or
celebrated. In fact, his paternity is recognized only through his associ-
ation with and proximity to his pregnant partner. How often do we
ask men about their feelings, concerns, and hopes about fatherhood?
    The conventions and practices surrounding pregnancy and child-
birth in our society—in contrast to those in more "primitive" cul-
tures, for example—provide American men with neither the activities
nor the rituals to help them feel important and included in the pregnancy process or to guide them through their own rites of passage into
new fatherhood. We must encourage and include men in prenatal
visits, childbirth classes, baby showers, labor and delivery, and

SUSAN LIRAKIS NICOLAY

immediate postpartum contact with their new children. We must broaden our concept of bonding to incorporate ways for both fathers and mothers to bond with their children before they are born as well as after. But underlying all of this, we must understand that fathers are pregnant, too!

Pregnant Fathers

Whether he realizes it or not, conception and pregnancy trigger a complex psychological process in a man as well as in a woman. An expectant father's responses to pregnancy may be more subtle and certainly less visible than his partner's. Indeed, he may make no connection between his changing moods and new fatherhood. Nevertheless, his metamorphosis is very real and very powerful. How he adjusts to his pregnancy will have a significant impact on his relationship with his partner, his children, and on the quality of his family's life.

As pregnancy progresses and men feel their child's "presence," they begin to see themselves differently—not so much as sons but as fathers. Pregnant fathers begin to reassess their interests, needs, goals, and abilities. As one father said: "I'm realizing the importance of what I am to my child, of how he sees me and what he learns and doesn't learn from me. I think about the kind of atmosphere I want him to grow up in. I want him to feel free to be what he wants. So, I'm trying hard to be the best person I can be." Becoming a parent means we must grow up ourselves, and quickly.

Expectant and new fathers, like their partners, often experience an array of feelings. They may feel ambivalent, envious, and left out; bewildered at times, and confident, proud, and self-assured at others. A pregnant father's most difficult task may be finding ways to feel meaningfully involved with his developing and young child. "Sympathy symptoms"—the weight gain, nausea, loss of appetite, and moodiness often reported by men during pregnancy—may well be expressions of this need to share the pregnancy and parenthood.

Feeling frustrated in his attempts to relate to the pregnancy or tired from attending to his partner's changing moods and needs, a pregnant father may feel resentful and alone, without any real appreciation for his own growth process or needs. Without the awareness of these pregnancy dynamics or the skills to communicate their feelings and needs directly, pregnant fathers may deal with their emotions less than satisfactorily by "taking a back seat," thus perpetuating their image and sense of themselves as outsiders, or by overworking or becoming overly involved in activities outside the home.

Getting to Know Your Child in Utero

Fathers can begin to establish a special and intimate connection with their child in utero, and at the same time dispel feelings of envy and exclusion, by reading about their unborn child's weekly development; learning about prenatal nutrition and serving as a health consultant to their pregnant partner; attending visits with obstetricians or midwives and listening to their child's heartbeat; and taking special time to "be alone" with their child—touching, kissing, visualizing, talking to their child, and noticing activity patterns such as hiccups and kicking. They can research childbirth classes, birthing options, and hospital delivery policies as well as "get the nest ready"—fix, build, and plan for their child's arrival. Talking with other fathers can be a valuable source of information and reassurance, as can playing with young infants and baby-sitting children of different ages.

Adjusting to Parenthood

Whatever your reactions are to becoming a parent, it is important that you give them expression. Realize that feelings are neither good nor bad, right nor wrong; they just are! Remember, too, that feelings are transitory, not permanent. Even the most unpleasant feelings can fade when shared and responded to empathetically. Holding in feelings and needs can lead only to frustration, upset, and alienation. Don't assume your partner knows what you are thinking or wanting. Conversely, don't assume he or she can't understand what you are going through.

Pregnancy is a time of heightened emotions and changing needs and routines for both of you. Make opportunities to share your thoughts and feelings with each other. You may be surprised (and relieved) to find yourselves dealing with the same issues. If finding time together seems difficult, schedule time together: it's that important! As one father told me after the birth of his child: "It's really important for a woman to make a man feel at ease during pregnancy—to help him realize that he's wanted. A man has a tendency to get kind of lost in the shuffle and not be as important a person as he was before. I needed more attention than I got. If I had been more vocal, probably my wife would have been more understanding. . . but I kind of held it inside."

Parenting as Partners
Both of you will go through your own unique creative process in becoming parents. At times during pregnancy and throughout parenthood, your paths will merge; at others, they will diverge. New fathers may need to be reminded that they are still loved and valued. New mothers may need to be reassured that their partners will be patient and understanding of their changes. Both of you will need to feel the other's warmth and support to help you develop a strong and lasting bond with each other and with your children.

Celebrate and ritualize your pregnancy in ways that are enjoyable and have meaning for both of you. This may mean attending movies about childbirth; discussing books; sharing hopes, dreams, childhood memories, and stories; keeping journals; relaxing and visualizing together; going out to a favorite restaurant; playing together; or spending romantic evenings together. Share your ideas about good parenting—your "should's" and "shouldn't's." Discuss your expectations for yourself and each other as parents. Ask practical questions such as: Who will work? Who will care for the infant? Who will read, feed, cook, clean, and discipline? Talk about your changing sex life.

When intercourse is uncomfortable or undesirable, find alternatives for expressing your love and needs for physical contact and closeness.

Parenting begins with conception, not childbirth. Pregnancy and parenting are two-person experiences. Remember, you are both becoming parents, and you need each other. Remember, too, that good parenting has nothing to do with gender. Parenting is a way of transmitting our knowledge, understanding, beliefs, and feelings to our children—a way, also, of expanding our personal horizons through caring, acceptance, involvement, and commitment.

The intensity and expression of our "parenting feelings" may fluctuate at different times in our lives. Still, the desire to parent and the satisfaction gained from partaking in our children's growth is as natural and important a part of being a man as of being a woman. Allow parenthood to deepen your relationship with yourself, your partner, and your children.

2

SUPPORTING THE SUPPORTING FATHER

Ken Druck

The experience of watching your wife labor, helping her breathe, and seeing the beautiful miracle of new life emerging is almost overwhelming, no matter how many times you have done it as a father. But the second time around, I knew what to expect. I knew more about helping Karen, both emotionally and physically. I was more prepared to be with her as she laughed, cried, and was joyful. I also knew more about how I would feel in the moments after I held my new daughter for the first time.

After Karen was comfortable and tiny Stephie was resting peacefully on her stomach, I went out of the room and fell into the arms of my best friend, Terry. Having coached Karen through labor and delivery, I could finally express my own emotions. I laughed and cried while Terry held me. When I returned to Karen and Stephie, I was able to give more emotionally than I had after the birth of my first daughter, because I had made sure that someone would be there for *me* to lean on. Karen, knowing that I had been with our friend Terry and that he was there to share my feelings, had one less thought on her mind. Having someone there to support me made a wonderful difference for all of us.

When my first daughter was born in 1975, the hospital barely tolerated my presence in the delivery room. I felt as if I was in everyone's way. My roles of helper and comforter were even partly taken over by people who were there because it was their job to be there. Karen and I arrived in the labor room and were just beginning to settle in, when I was asked to leave while hospital personnel "prepped" her. I resented the feeling of being an intruder in a feminine experience orchestrated by a male doctor. It also seemed to me that, in many ways, the authoritative presence of the doctor was a modern compensation for the traditionally missing father.

Today, both in and out of hospitals, fathers are given much more recognition as partners. But even alternative birthing usually centers around the mother and the child and casts the father in a secondary role.

Birth is an intense experience for fathers as well as mothers. While we do not experience the physical part of labor, we are involved in a very real process that can frustrate, elate, and exhaust us. Meeting our children for the first time is nearly overwhelming emotionally.

The magical intensity that is a part of this meeting is more than most men ever imagine. After months of sharing the ups and downs of his wife's pregnancy, and then a labor during which he may feel helpless, the new father, who has not had the intimate contact with the unborn baby that the mother has had, faces the awesome and wrenching realization that this baby is real, physically real, and now part of his life. The sudden, separate reality of the child is often over-whelming.

Holding his newborn child is an emotional experience that he never forgets. This swelling of emotion can be difficult for a man who is uncomfortable with his strongest feelings or unwilling to ask for support and understanding. But even if a man is fairly comfortable with his own emotions, fulfilling his role as birth coach almost demands that he hold them in.

For a long time, men had little more to do with the birth of their children other than waiting, pacing, and handing out cigars. Yet even in an age that seems to foster father involvement, many men are reluc-tant to admit or even consider what they are going through. Men who remain a pillar of strength for everyone around them through the entire birthing process deny themselves a chance to be fully involved.

In the words of a man whose wife had been through a difficult labor: "We were so exhausted. All of us. The midwife Dana and my wife Loren looked as tired as two women can look. I had never seen a human being work so hard. My own knees were weak, and I trembled when I held my daughter. My throat became so tight I couldn't speak, and I kept swallowing, afraid that I was about to cry. My wife looked at me and smiled a beautiful smile. If I could have cried, I'd probably have felt better. But I didn't want to upset her. Later, two of my friends admitted that they had felt the same way."

We are all intensely aware that the birthing mother needs emotional

JOHN SCHOENWALTER

and physical help and support. It is one of the precious moments in any man's life to be part of his wife's support team. But a new father needs support, too. He needs to think about who can give him that support and to anticipate the upcoming experience in a way that is usually reserved for expectant mothers.

If we want to involve ourselves equally in parenting, the logical place to begin is at the birth. We become fathers on the same day that our wives become mothers. Emotional support is as vital for us as it is for them.

By remaining aloof, at least outwardly, from the emotion that surrounds a birth, a man may set the stage for emotionally distancing himself from other events to come in family life. Expressing his feelings at the birthing can begin a process that enriches marriage and parenting, as well as the lives of his children, immensely.

A prebirth gathering of men, where stories of births are told by men who experienced them, can provide invaluable preparation for any new father. As we share stories and feelings, a pool of support is built. Fathers who begin by supporting one another are in a better position to exchange "trade secrets" and support as the years pass. Parenting is a challenge that is best met with support and sharing.

The swell of feelings at birth sets the tone for an unfolding of emotion as our children grow. They need to know us as we truly are. With whom can we be as silly and playful and funny as with our kids? There is an implicit permission in our society for a man to be emotionally free around his children, to play and be childlike.

My friend Terry told me years later that by trusting him with all my emotions when Stephie was born, I had given him a precious gift that deepened our already close friendship. When a man includes his friends in the birth experience, whether they are present or simply available afterward for a time of retelling and supportive hugs, he truly shares one of the most important experiences of his lifetime.

I am not an unusual man. That is to say, I received the same basic emotional training in my early life that most men received. I could have "machoed" my way through a second birth. I could have remained outwardly calm and supportive for Karen and handled my own feelings by simply stifling them at the moment, then diluting them as time went on. I might even have been congratulated for my strength and emotional reserve. But I chose not to do that, and with this choice, I paved the way for a fuller emotional life for myself as a man, a husband, and a father.

3

DEAREST PAPA

Victor LaCerva

Dearest Papa,
At times like this, full of overwhelming changes and intensity, fathers can begin to feel confused. I know you're suffering from sleep deprivation, and I want to reassure you that this situation is just another transition—short, but demanding. Please relax, take a few deep breaths, and let me share with you some important facts that you may not know about me.

First, let me tell you that I've grown much wiser since 1926, when James Watson wrote the following: "All we have to start with in building a human being is a lively squirming bit of flesh, capable of making a few simple responses such as movements of the hands and arms and fingers and toes, crying and smiling, making certain sounds with its throat . . . parents take this raw material and begin to fashion it in ways to suit themselves."

As in much of the natural world, here a universe of individual variation lies within the boundaries of a general principle. The observation of different infant states of being began the process of understanding us. How I move from state to state—deep and light sleep, drowsy, awake-alert, awake-active, and crying, and the amount of time I spend in each—reflects my emerging personality. I have been around for forty weeks already, you know, and have had lots of time to develop tools for interacting with the world around me.

I can see quite well, about 20/200 on a standard eye chart test, and have done so since my eyes were completely formed and open at about seven months in utero. The optimal focusing distance for my visual field is about twelve to fifteen inches, which just happens to be the distance from my eyes to mom's when I am nursing. I prefer the image of a face to any other visual stimulus. I guess people still think I don't see because I can fix my eyes on something for only short periods of time. I'll get better at that; in the meantime, you must trust me to see what I need to.

I've been hearing from about the sixth month of fetal life. I often feel calm now when you play that soft piece on the piano that mom liked to hear when she was pregnant. My whole body moves in microrhythm to adult speech. I can turn my head toward the source of a sound, though this movement is subtle, and you really must watch me closely to catch it. I can, of course, distinguish your voice from mom's and both of yours' from strangers'.

I have a fair amount of taste and smell discrimination. I can recognize the smell of my mother and distinguish her scent from that of another woman. I like the smell of fruit but grimace at the smell of rotten eggs. My facial muscles have been capable of expressing the full range of human emotions since the eleventh week of my life inside the womb.

It is very different being out here in the world—so many new stimuli, and so much to adjust to. That's why I sneeze a lot and have hiccups and sensitive, peeling skin; my body is reacting to this environment. Anything that reminds me of my former state comforts me. Swaddling gives me the sense of boundaries that I had late in pregnancy, when there wasn't much extra room in my mother's uterus. Constant motion and rocking remind me of the gentle undulations I felt for so many months within the womb, and body contact brings me back to the intimate feelings of being inside mom.

Despite the fact that "infant" is derived from the Latin *infans*, meaning "not speaking," I do vocalize quite a bit. My fussing will, within weeks, become cooing, and then in a few months, babbling. My early speech is practice and preparation for learning language. We infants vary a great deal in the amount of our individual early verbal expression. But the more you talk with me, the more I'll begin to respond back.

So, Papa, I've given you an overview of some of the things I can do. The instinct for survival is the key to understanding me. From the time when the placenta forms between myself and mom, there is a union of cells derived from each of us. Normally, my cells would be rejected by her body as foreign. In some way that we do not understand, the placenta is fully accepted immunologically. I take what I need nutritionally through this vital organ, sometimes at her expense. I also get her body to process the waste products of my metabolism.

Under the influence of pregnancy hormones, mom's breasts begin to produce milk, which will come as I stimulate the process by my sucking. This system will become so sensitive to my needs that just the thought or sight of me can stimulate the letdown of milk in preparation for a feeding. I seem at times to want to suck everything, but my suck overdrive is geared to produce plenty of food for my early rapid growth. Like the milk of other mammals, breast milk is a species-specific, nutritionally balanced, complete survival food. The immunologic protection it offers is truly astounding. Colostrum, the first milk, is rich in electrolytes and higher in protein than later milk. This assures nutritional adequacy in those first few days when my intake of breast milk is minimal.

I am a survivor because I use my body energy efficiently. As you have noticed, when I am calm, I am totally relaxed. I sleep from sixteen to twenty hours a day, which gives you and mom some intermittent breaks from my intensity. Many of my awake periods are at night, when the external stimuli are quieter and more womblike. This pattern of night waking helped our hunter-gatherer ancestors to survive, since daytime crying would have attracted predators while they were away from the safety of a cave or other nighttime shelter. My pattern of sleeping more during the day was safer for them and allows you to get some things done.

It has been shown that as evolution has progressed, species with more developed brains have greater proportions of rapid eye movement (REM) sleep. About 70 percent of my sleep as a newborn is REM type, which provided lots of mental activity in the womb. As external stimulation increases over the next months and I become more conscious of the outer world in many ways, my REM sleep will decrease to the adult level of about 20 percent.

Just as I can be totally relaxed, my energies can mobilize quickly in an all-out effort to communicate a need. In other words, I can cry like hell to let you know that something is wrong. Crying is not unique to humans, for many infant mammals use this powerful survival tool to communicate with their parents. There also exists a group crying phenomenon, whereby newborn distress spreads to other infants to attract even more attention. This has evolved in older humans into joint attention, or the tendency to look where others are looking. This is a mechanism to rapidly spread awareness of danger, or of a novel stimulus, among a group. Try not looking up when others are

MICHAEL WEISBROT

doing so on a busy urban street, and you will sense this powerful drive.

I am born with the neurologically complex ability to tune out when there is constant stimuli—thus the legendary sleep-inducing magic of a car ride or the sound of the vacuum cleaner. Otherwise, I would be at the mercy of all new environmental stimuli and would be quickly overwhelmed. In this way I conserve energy and save my attention for when there is something interesting going on. If you clap your hands, I will respond at first with a startle. This response will diminish with each successive clap; by the third clap, I will not react at all. This exercise illustrates conservation of energy by limitation of new stimuli, a process geared to produce learning at an optimum pace. A beautiful design, don't you think?

I am also programmed for social interaction. In these first weeks of life, I will alter my sleep-awake cycle so that my periods of quiet alertness will coincide with your more attentive times. I will mold my body into your arms with a built-in cuddling response, thus responding in a positive physical way to your attention. You already understand the importance of body contact with me. Touch is the earliest functioning sensory system for all mammals. It is an important form of stimulation and pleasure throughout life but especially for the young of a species. From the licking of newborn goats and the grooming of baby primates to the pattern of touching observed in humans with their newborns, touch seems to play an important species-specific role in stimulation and early socialization.

I prefer to look at faces, seeking them out from an array of other stimuli and looking at them longer than anything else. In the early weeks, I concentrate on the periphery of your face. This focus gradually shifts inward, culminating in prolonged eye contact by six weeks of age. Also, about this time, just when you think that this difficult yet wondrous period of constant, intense caretaking will never end, my first smile will wash away your fatigue, delight you, and prepare you for the next phase of my life. I smile back at anyone who smiles at me, since they may be important to my future survival. This simple gesture strongly reinforces social interaction.

Pregnancy prepared you in some ways for the first six weeks after birth. The excitement of feeling me move in the womb, mom's frequent night wakings in the last months, the nesting urge through which you created a physical space for me, the anticipation of not knowing exactly when I would arrive—these are all part of nature's plan to help you welcome me. However, by six weeks postpartum you are ready for more reinforcement, and my smile gives it. It will soon be used not only to reinforce but also to initiate social interaction. As with physical stimuli, I set the pace of social development, looking away or tuning out when I've had enough.

I am also born with certain motor reflexes that are useful for survival. When placed face down on a surface, I can turn my head to the side in order to breathe, although my neck muscles are not yet strong enough to fully support my head. Stimulation of the side of my mouth causes me to turn my head and root in that direction. Gradually, I gain more skilled use of my body, starting with my head and proceeding to my toes. This is logical and survival-oriented. For example, my head control develops before I can reach for objects. It's difficult to have good eye-hand coordination if your head is bouncing around unsupported.

Ontogeny recapitulates phylogeny: the development of an individual organism mimics the evolutionary progression of a species. Very early in my fetal development, I looked quite fishlike. I had "gill"- type arches and pouches of primitive cells which ultimately became different tissues and organs. At birth, I still have some simian motor memories. Both my startle and grasp reflexes reflect survival movements that enabled infant monkeys to quickly and automatically latch onto a moving mother.

Papa, there is much you do not understand about newborns. I have shown you how much we can do and how, prepared by millions of years of genetic memory for life on our planet, we manipulate our environment to ensure our survival. But there is more. I am a catalyst for change within your life. You and I are meant to grow together, for a driving force of evolution is the interaction of parents with their young.

We newborns are powerful, yet nonthreatening. Our unpredictable nature stimulates your curiosity. Adults are drawn to infants and want to interact with them in an uninhibited fashion. When you pick me up, you tend to place me on the left side of your chest, where I can sometimes hear the soothing rhythm of your heartbeat. Most paintings of the Madonna and Child picture this position. Adults speak to infants in a high-pitched voice (which we prefer), spouting *goo goo gah gahs* as easily as they talk with an old friend. This later becomes baby talk, a complex language with its own rules and phrases, practiced universally and unconsciously by humans. Accompanying this are exaggerated facial expressions, synchronized with verbalization.

Adults have a well-defined sense of personal space. Newborn and young infants do not and will tolerate being touched or picked up by a stranger or being placed within inches of someone else's face. Even prolonged eye contact, which adults commonly avoid, is lavished on infants. Watch your friends as they relate to me. You will observe complex, instinctual behavior, which I trigger in them to promote my survival.

Watch me. I can teach you to live in the present. I am aware of my body's needs and prioritize their fulfillment. I sleep when I am tired, demand to be fed when hungry, and later, when I am toddling, I will release stress through my tantrums. I don't need a computer to plot my biorhythms; I just dance to my own circadian tune. I will demand attention as strongly as I request food and will tailor that attention to set my own pace at learning. I seek new stimuli and learn something every day. Because I view the world through the eyes of the present, there is always much that is new.

I also put you in touch with your unconscious through my night wakings, affording you multiple opportunities for remembering your dreams. The sleep deprivation and the intensity of the first weeks of my life combine to induce in you a definitely altered state of consciousness. And, of course, I constantly trigger your emotional life, serving as a mirror within which you can see your deepest self, if you are willing to look. As early as the beginning of pregnancy, Papa, I gave you the opportunity to examine your fears. Would I be normal? Would the birth go well? I now test the limits of your patience, releasing your anger at times and giving you more opportunities for self-awareness. And another great circle begins to complete itself, as I constantly trigger memories and raise questions about how you were parented.

I am your unconscious connection to that collective flow of humanity that is unspoken, yet very much felt. Don't I sense immediately when someone who is uncomfortable holding me picks me up? Don't I feel and react to tension in a room? Much that is unknown in the world can be explored through the key that infants provide, for we are free of the consensual reality that at times imprisons you. We are the repositories of archetypal wisdom, the keepers of the untapped genetic potential of our species.

In sum, I offer you pure experience, lots of practice in being in the present, a taste of communication with the unconscious, and constant insight into your emotional life, along with much joy and laughter to fill your days and nights. As I emerge from the safety of the womb, I invite you to transcend the boundaries of your self-awareness. Remember that ideas, over time, have a way of attaining biological reality. Surrender to the flow of life that I represent. When you are with me, be conscious of your thoughts and actions, for they wlll provide the feedback you need for growth. Relax, enjoy and trust your feelings and intuitions. Life provides, for both of us.

All my love,
Gina Rae Nuvia

4

How Parenting Civilizes Us

Robert Millar

"Honey!" My wife's urgent whisper penetrated slowly through the sweet peacefulness of my predawn slumbers. "Honey, wake up! I think it's time!"

"Time for what?" I mumbled, reluctant to pull myself away from that delicious drowsiness that graces my sleep only in the early hours of the morning.

"Time to go to the hospital. I think the baby's coming!"

A surge of adrenaline shocked me into keen awareness. Bolting upright, I snapped on the bedside lamp. "H-how do you know?"

"Don't worry, I *know!*" she declared, with a confident smile.

That was good enough for me. Twenty minutes later we were in the hospital labor room, putting every ounce of training we had absorbed from our Lamaze classes into practice. Several hours after that, we were the ecstatic parents of a beautiful baby boy.

In that instant, the quality of our lives was dramatically altered. We would never again be the same.

"So, what's new?" you ask. At first glance, nothing. I guess just about all the parents I've ever spoken with have freely admitted that having a child significantly changed their lives. The kinds of changes most people mention have to do with things like dramatically increased responsibilities, the overcoming of personal preferences as they rearrange their lives to accommodate the new family member, and the joyous rewards of witnessing the growth of a human being. But there is a subtler and even more significant change that occurs when we have children. It is a change that may well be a key element in the establishment and maintenance of a civilized society. Parenthood increases our capacity to love.

I consider myself to be a fairly ordinary person. Like most people, I feel warmly disposed toward my friends and relatives (most of them, anyway). I love my parents, and I am head over heels in love with my wife. But I have never before experienced anything like the overwhelming kind of love that I feel for my son. What makes it so remarkable is that it is so utterly selfless. From the moment I first saw him I knew, without a doubt, that I would do anything to protect him and ensure his greatest welfare and happiness. Of course, this kind of dedication has also been present to varying degrees in my other relationships, but never before with such intensity, consistency, or suddenness. In retrospect, it seems that I built up love and commitment in other relationships over a period of time during which I got to know and trust the people concerned. But the parent-child relationship is unique in my experience, in that I felt committed the instant my son was born. It was truly love at first sight. Even now, over two years later, I am still struck by the quality of that love and its continuing impact on my life.

I remember carrying him from the delivery room to the nursery, awestruck by the birth experience and the strong feelings of love and protectiveness experienced for the first time just moments before. I could hardly give him over to the nurse for the weighing and measuring ritual. I was shocked to find how passionately protective I felt about this new person in my life, whom I didn't really even know yet!

Protectiveness and unconditional love are the recurring themes I hear whenever I talk with other new parents about the nature of their feelings toward their children. They are profoundly deep feelings, which I don't think most of us ever fully understand or experience until we have children. They are feelings that mark the turning point in most of our lives from being essentially self-centered to putting the welfare of another person before our own.

In our preparental years, our "footloose and fancy-free" years, most of us think we have a pretty fair understanding of what it means to love someone. We are aware of warm feelings for our family and friends, and we thrill to the effervescent feelings that accompany "falling in love" with someone. But it is only when we are face-to-face with our first child that we may begin to realize that much of our understanding of love has revolved around our own self-interest. The fact that the parent-child relationship differs significantly from this pattern is echoed in the words of one mother I spoke to: "To give to someone so completely, without thoughts of any return, is so unique and such an honor."

and such an honor."

This aspect of loving—giving "without thoughts of any return"—comes as somewhat of a surprise. Most of us have no idea we possess such a powerful, latent capacity. The tapping of this resource, a naturally occurring component of parenting, gives us the courage and stamina to face the challenges of parenthood.

The implications of this experience of selfless giving are more far-reaching than first meets the eye. Since the birth of my son, I have a different attitude toward children in general than I ever had before. I am embarrassed to admit that I used to think they were cute when they were well-behaved and obnoxious when they weren't. They were sources of irritation to me in restaurants and theaters, and they asked too many questions. Because I didn't have any children of my own, they were somehow not fully "real" to me. It was easy to objectify them, to depersonalize them, to stay uninvolved with them. Now that I am a parent, I am slowly beginning to feel for all children. Some strange alchemy is occurring through which all children are becoming, in a sense, "my" children. My former lack of involvement with them is giving way to an increasing concern for their welfare, wherever they may be.

While thumbing through a recent issue of *Newsweek* magazine, I saw a picture of a father carrying his young, mortally wounded son out of a war-torn sector of Lebanon. The look of anguish on the father's face and the look of innocent incredulity on the face of the dying child evoked an intense horror and outrage in me that I have never before experienced in reading about world affairs. Suddenly, I could fully emphathize with their pain, I could fully understand the tremendous injustice of the situation, and these feelings cut me deeply.

Norman Cousins has written, "The good education is one that can help us to move out beyond the narrow and calcifying confines of the ego so that we can identify ourselves compassionately with the mainstream of humanity." I never realized how much my education had been lacking until my son was born. Since his arrival, I have learned more about the nature of the human being and the nature of love than I ever suspected existed.

As I apply this knowledge to my daily life, I find that just as I now have a different regard for children than I once had, I also am beginning to experience greater understanding and concern for all people.

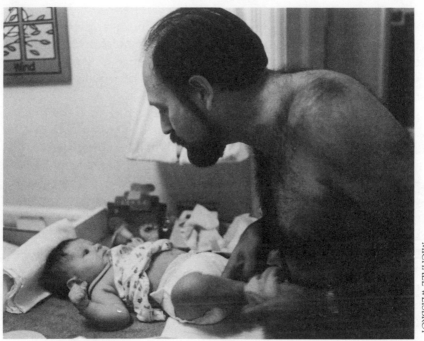

MICHAEL WEISBROT

In much the same way as all children are becoming "my own," all men and women are becoming my "family." A new sense of camaraderie and compassion is slowly developing. Whereas before I felt a sense of separation and isolation from "all those other people," now I realize how much we have in common.

It is in this way that parenthood can play a key role in the creation of a civilized society. We have the ability to extend our newly awakened feelings of love and selflessness beyond the context of the parent-child relationship, where they seem to arise of their own accord, and to establish similar sympathetic connections with all those around us. Society depends upon just such connections for its existence. In *Webster's Third New International Dictionary*, one definition of the word "society" is "a group of people who possess the quality or state of being connected." Society, therefore, is not just a group of people living together. It is a group of people living together with significant bonds to one another, bonds which ensure a sense of cohesiveness and belonging—a sense of the familiar. (As a matter of fact, the word "familiar" derives from the word "family," with all its

associations of mutual concern and support.) The experience of
parenting is particularly beneficial, in that it provides us with the
direct experience of putting someone else's welfare before our own in a
new and concentrated way. It gives us direct experience of how the
process works. For once in our lives, we do not find ourselves saying,
"After me, you come first."

   I don't think the feelings I've described are unique to my experience;
I'm sure they are felt by most parents on some level. What has been
particularly thrilling to me is the dawning of a new, experiential
knowledge of the possibilities implied by these feelings. It is part of the
glory of the parenting experience that we are presented with an
opportunity to break free of the restricted boundaries of our private
worlds and to begin to embrace more and more of life. The new kind
of grief I suffered when I looked at the picture of the father and son in
Lebanon, the kind of joy I now feel when I see other parents pushing
their children on the swings at the park—these feelings have awakened in me an expansive sense of connectedness, a kind of fellow-
feeling for these people which makes me feel bonded to them in ways I
never felt before. The more sympathetically I feel involved with them,
the more I am likely to take their welfare into account in the conduct
of my daily life. The more that people mean something to me, the
more inclined I will be to act considerately and conscientiously in
every sphere of activity my life touches, from domestic relations and
business activities to international affairs. As a result, in my own
small way, I cannot help but be more of a force for good and harmony
in the world.

PART II:
FATHERING AND SELF

5

Man, Husband, and Father

Peter J. Dorsen

I became a husband at thirty-seven and a father at thirty-eight, later in life than such events occur for most men. Marriage and children have made tremendous changes in my life—but, I would say, changes for the better. My wife and daughters symbolize my first real emotional commitment as a man. Indeed, I have joked to some that my final predicament, to be surrounded by four women, is just reward for my womanizing years. Now with three girls—Bria, who is almost eight; Gabriella, or Gabi for short, almost four; and Katarina, our one-year-old Christmas baby—there is an entirely new category of clothes on laundry day: pink.

I have evolved from a carefree bachelor who could drop his undies wherever they fell to a committed husband and father. Now I know everything about sleepless nights; the fear of whether I can provide adequately for my family's needs; and mundane experiences like dropping children off at school, picking them up for piano lessons, and sitting through endless hours of dance class. There is no better accolade that I could hear than Gabi saying soulfully, "You're the best daddy I ever had."

The solitude is gone. Actually, perhaps a better way to describe my bachelor years is as periods of loneliness interspersed with episodes of uncommitted intimacy or so-called serial monogamy. Not bad, but my present life-style is far preferable. I am lucky to be surrounded by women; their femaleness is counterpoint to my maleness.

Similar to most men of my era, before I became a father I had no prior experience with babies. I had never baby-sat and had no brothers or sisters. I recall the frustration and fear I felt at the outset in looking after each of Susy's and my children. Gradually, I gained confidence as each child seemed to accept my tenderness. So what if the chest I offered was hairy; it was warm and caring. Bit by bit, I dis-covered I was capable of being masculine *and* sensitive, realized that assuming roles I had associated exclusively with mothers or wives made me no less a man. Today, I appreciate the approving glances of women when I have one child on my back and another in the stroller. I love the little acts of caring I used to associate with mothering, such as chopping Kata's spaghetti or crumbling a roll for her, wiping mouths, and escorting kids to the bathroom. All the statistics show that married men like myself are more content, live longer, and have a lower suicide rate. I sometimes wonder, though, with all the craziness of life with children, whether it is the length of one's life that is so important after all.

Our basement sauna, a four-by-seven-foot space, offers a good yardstick for how my family has grown and changed. Before children (B.C.), a sauna, followed by a relaxing cool shower, was a leisurely, pleasant way to let heat and steam take the stress out of my body. My main concerns now are undressing three little kids, preparing a cool bath for the youngest, or hustling them out to the shower so they won't fry. Gone are the solitude and quiet that once characterized the sauna experience.

Sexuality is a big part of being a man but, in my case, one only gradually understood. Unselfish lovemaking is something I learned only after entering a committed relationship with Susy. Another new aspect of my sexual experience, one that was never a necessity before I had children, is patience. The intimate breast-feeding relationship Susy has with our youngest child meets her intimacy needs; it can also sometimes be overwhelming physically. There are just some times when she can't deal with anyone else pulling at her body. It is very important during this period for us to communicate our individual needs. I may tell Susy that I feel sexually frustrated, but it is equally important for her to help me understand all the physical demands on her. I have found that masturbation can be a reasonably satisfying way to relieve sexual tension. It does not have to be a secret habit or be regarded as shameful, since it can help cope with those times when physical intimacy is impossible.

Sexual spontaneity is not always possible for many couples, espe-cially when they have several young children running in and out of their bedroom. My wife and I informally schedule our sex in advance; we talk about it with each other. It is always fun to discover that my mate is in the mood for sex as well. In our case, it is crucial not to postpone our liaison much after our children go to sleep. Locking the door guarantees that we will not have any surprise visitors.

We are also comfortable having our children join us in our bed before they go to sleep or when they wake up. This allows us to share our own closeness with our children. While the girls are still sleepy, their innocence and softness counteract any stress that lingers from those wakeful moments when they are on overdrive. I confess to some ambivalence toward having children in my bed all night, yet I try to remain sensitive to their needs for security and intimacy. And there is something very comforting about all of us snuggling together after a hard day.

It is also vitally important for my wife and I to schedule one night out a week. Usually, we prefer to have dinner at a comfortable restaurant in order to have quiet time together. Our time out is an acceptable escape from the children (who usually prefer a favorite sitter over their parents anyway). There, by candlelight and with a nice glass of wine, our date becomes an opportunity to rediscover ourselves and the reasons why we are sharing our lives. It is during our times alone that Susy and I discuss how we want to parent our children. We may also share frustrations from other areas of our lives, trying to understand and remain sympathetic to each other. Although we sometimes must search for the spark that brought us together in the first place and that produced the kids who are driving us to distraction, these times provide the chance to confirm that we still love one another.

As men, fathers, and husbands, we wear many hats. We may be a professional one moment and a volunteer dad the next. It is important for us to understand that "you are *who* you are, not *what* you are." Hopefully, expectations of us as fathers and husbands are changing. It is a mistake to believe that only women have the correct genes to nurture, or that they have an exclusive handle on intimacy. That is to say, we, like women, are now allowed to share in nurturing and to be sensitive.

Carl Jung wrote that the first part of a man's life is often one of action, and that the second half is a time for introspection. At the age of forty-two, after eleven years of private practice as a doctor, I became a free-lance writer. My new profession has allowed me to set my own hours. As a result, I can spend the early part of each day with my

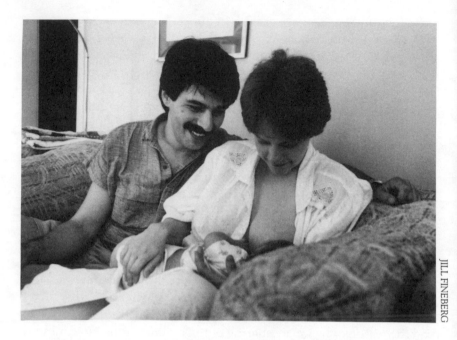

JILL FINEBERG

children and then write all afternoon. My life as a free-lancer gives me control of my own time.

When I began writing at home, the problem was not sitting down to work but rather leaving my study and stopping work. In our culture, men are identified by their profession. Their work becomes who they are. We are also admired for how much we earn. But how much admiration do we get based on the amount of time we spend with our children? It is becoming increasingly evident that we have everything to gain by being there for our kids. The adage, "Children need more dad and less mom," is so very important.

During the first year of my early "retirement," as it were, I became involved on a weekly basis with each daughter at her school. For a year, I attended a weekly group at Gabi's preschool in which I was the only male. Because of our trips to and from school and our times together—Gabi on my lap singing while her teacher played the guitar—my daughter and I established a mutual comfort level and became close. I also volunteered to teach reading weekly in Bria's first-grade classroom, which gave me an opportunity to experience her learning situation firsthand.

Ours is an increasingly complex and fast-paced society. Most of us have work and economic pressures that influence how we spend our day. Financial paranoia affects most of us, and many of us must work at the banal or meaningless. It is the rare father who has even the option of spending extra time with his children. However, those little extra efforts, whether they are a weekly dinner with one's spouse or volunteering a half-day at a child's school, may be one of the most effective ways to tell other people in our family, "I love you." Giving that little extra to our children and companions can help redefine who we are as fathers, husbands, and men. Once we can shed the trappings of professionalism and strip down to the basic role of "Susy's husband" or "Bria's dad," we begin to find out who we really are.

There is a legion of stereotypes of men and women which are, fortunately, finally beginning to break down. I, for one, certainly found that I needed all the support I could get from my wife to begin assuming responsibility for each new child who came into our life. The only diapers I had ever changed were during my medical residency many years before. But now I have discovered how good intimacy feels when Kata nestles up to me when I cradle a bottle for her. She is comfortable with me, a male, and I know that the sensitivity I have for this tiny creature I helped make is masculine as well as feminine.

However, being a dad and husband has not always been easy for me. As my wife and I began having children, I found I needed more time away from the family, perhaps as an escape from the pressure I felt parenting and husbanding. At 6:00 a.m., I would often jog off to my local health club to lift weights. This meant I was not around for breakfast. That program worked at the time but is history now. Since the birth of our third child, I find it more important to sit around the breakfast table. I relish the opportunity to feed Kata, our new baby. Such an attitude change is perhaps the result of my successful entry into what Jung saw as the contemplative part of my life. The amount of love I feel for each of our children continues to astound me, especially since I struggled so hard against commitment earlier in my life.

It is common in our society to see women who have completed their primary nurturing role enter the professional fields of law, business, or research and begin scaling the corporate ladder. Similarly, many older men have begun to pursue new kinds of meaning in their lives. That may be why, two years ago, several middle-aged men and I formed a men's group. That group has been an opportunity for us to look at our lives, our careers, and our relationships together. With our wives and children quietly tucked away, ten of us meet monthly in one of our living rooms where we try to get beyond "the b.s." in our lives.

Each of us shares the joys or frustrations of his family relationships. We talk about job stress and male intimacy issues. Over time, we have gotten closer and shared secrets. I have found a great sense of comfort participating in these gatherings. At times, I have been afraid of this intimacy, but the interactions I have experienced within this group have helped me relate better and less fearfully to men outside it. The opportunity to take emotional risks has made this group more valuable for most of us.

It is little surprise that Michael McGill, in the *McGill Report on Male Intimacy* (New York: Harper and Row, 1985), challenges men's ability to be intimate. Our way of relating to one another and to others is often very superficial. Men struggle with the intimacy that women seem to handle naturally. But men have also seen one another as adversaries for a long time. Often we are competing for the same prizes in the arena of life. By contrast, women hug, kiss, and cry in front of one another. Yet today, many women are trying some of the bonding techniques that men have always taken for granted, such as playing ball, horseplay in the locker room, and hanging out with their buddies for a drink.

Men *do* struggle with intimacy. Perhaps it's safer to say that many men avoid intimacy. Our men's group has given us a chance to bring down the barriers that are culturally manufactured, to challenge attitudes such as, "Big boys don't cry." The members of the group care about each other. It is a place where it is acceptable to be sensitive, to show feelings, even to cry. At the beginning, I needed reassurance from several others that as a man, caring about others did not mean I was gay.

After I was married, it became easy to simply define myself as one woman's husband, asexual to the outside world. That another woman would perceive me as a sexual object was now out of the question. But one night, as I stood alone at the bar in my favorite bistro, I realized how ridiculous it was to think this way. Suddenly, I was uncomfortable in a place where, by day, I could spend hours reading or writing. My discomfort awakened me to the importance of my identity outside of my marriage.

Isn't it fascinating how two people in a mature relationship begin to assume each other's characteristics? Some joke about how partners even come to resemble each other physically. Similarly, it is easy for children to see their parents as a unit rather than as two separate people. It is important for children to know their parents as *people*, distinct from each other. It is vital for my children to know the wild and crazy part of my personality, the one that surfaces at the start of a ski race and, hopefully, is still there at the finish. I would be quick to agree with the pearl, "Setting a good example for your children takes all the fun out of middle age."

In relationships, it is also crucial to maintain your male identity and independence. I suspect that the inadvertent loss of some of my own sense of identity, initially through marriage and then exponentially with the birth of each new child, may have contributed to several recent bouts with depression. I would not be surprised if most men have a difficult time coping with the disparate demands of work, home, and family. It is a great challenge to find ample time to communicate with our mates or our children. In our home, we ask each child to "check in" as we sit around the dinner table. During these exchanges, we tell one another about our day and, in a sense, why we are special. This ritual helps bring the family together. It is a time for sharing and listening, but it also identifies each of us as individuals.

For me, masculine identity is made up of all the adjustments and compromises in family life. Male identity is sensitivity to one's wife and children, rather than "zoning out." I have learned to time my escapes from the house for running or skiing to the hours when one daughter is sleeping and the others are away at school. My own family participation offers me the opportunity to share all I know, as well as my values and feelings, with my children. As parents, we are our children's conduit to the world. We help them understand the complexities of life. Our children, in turn, appreciate everything we offer them, regardless of how inconsequential. They are like sponges, absorbing everything around them.

My identity as a male also means treating my wife as an equal and respecting what she is doing with her life and with the children. My life as a single person consumed the better part of my early years. Only since my marriage and the birth of my children have I begun to reach fulfillment as a male. As Kata snuggles up against my chest, I begin to understand what can be the essence of masculinity. I also realize I must have a certain amount of independence within my marriage. Some call such independent dependence "interdependence."

Crucial to growth in a relationship is that both partners give up control and stop trying to change the other. This is easy to say, tough to accomplish. Our maximum potential for growth will occur when we can finally commit to a permanent relationship of any kind. Being respectful and sensitive to our families and others defines what is truly good in all of us.

6

The Importance of Grief

Victor LaCerva

I watch the walls go up slowly. I don't want them there, but they seem to grow each day. Often I am too tired to protest, to make a stand and stop this withdrawal deep inside me. I am in pain, and the walls designed to protect me do not do their job for more than a short time.

The stress, fatigue, and intensity of babydom have taken their toll again. I miss my wife, my mate, my best friend, my lover. Where is she?

The only constant is change. I've been through this before, so I know that the situation does evolve. That realization gives little comfort now, though, as I struggle daily to create the time, energy, and space to connect with my wife. I am hungry to have time alone with her, to share myself fully. . . no, I don't mean sex, though I would welcome more of that as well. I mean, to speak more than a few sentences without the needs of the children interrupting. To subsist on more than the leftovers we bring each other at the end of the day. When the little ones are both finally asleep, the dishes done, the trash taken out, and basic preparations for another day of it all completed, there is precious little left.

I feel like a master juggler, practicing and focusing on the art of balance. I toss work, the children, my wife, and myself high into the air each day and trust that life will provide what is necessary to nurture. It is an exhausting, moment-to-moment skill, this juggling, and my expectations of how things should turn out often add to the difficulty. That is where the real work lies: within the conversations in my head. The work of achieving balance starts there and moves outward.

When my inner self can let go of its expectations, ask clearly for what it needs, and be grateful for all the goodness that already is, daily life seems to adjust itself and flow more easily. I stop seeking for

JILL FINEBERG

ultimate answers and final solutions and focus on little day-to-day improvements. I stop being married to who my wife isn't and appreci-ate more who she is.

Although we know better, most of us men still expect our mates to fill a hole in our souls. At those difficult times when we are not get-ting our needs met by our partners, we feel a great loss. If we do not express that loss and sadness, the walls go up, and with time become too strong to tear down.

After the births of both of my children, one of the ways I survived the difficult months of baby love, baby maintenance, and lack of physical contact with my wife was through the support I received from other men. They have consistently provided me with a safe space where I share my inner life. They listen without judgment. They share freely their own pain and difficulties. They inspire me to heal my inner child, and thus heal myself.

At the fifth annual New Mexico Men's Wellness Conference, we built a wailing wall. Over the course of two days, six sheets of plywood were filled with the words and phrases of pain that had been carried inside us for too long. At first, I wanted to write it all down, to preserve this essence of what had touched so many men so deeply. Instead, I read and pondered and felt, and the following poem emerged:

> There is something about the sound of a man crying that frightens me—
> those first moans of sadness that come from depths unfamiliar
> for too long
> perhaps the little boy in me cannot bear to know that there
> is pain in being a man—that those who hold my little hand,
> and protect me from the darkness, are also vulnerable.
> There is something about the sound of a man crying that makes
> me want to shout—
> that catching of the breath as painful groans emerge in spurts from the
> shaking body—
> part of me wants to scream, "Stop it! Grow up! Be strong!
> We all know life is hard without you reminding us," and thus
> create a wall of words to keep my own grief away.
> There is something about the sound of a man crying that
> compels me to hold him
> the waves of wailing sorrow that drown attempts to speak,
> sentences broken apart by the storm's fury, his body
> collapsing into the moment
> the father in me wants to comfort with my arms, simply being
> there, saying nothing, offering a safe space of love and
> acceptance.
> There is something about the sound of a man crying that heals me
> those soft snifflings as the face relaxes, the deep sighs and
> the palpable calm of release that signal another part of another wound is
> healed again
> and the man I am is filled with hope by all these sounds,
> especially when they are my own.

When I allow myself to actively acknowledge the sadness I experience from not having enough time with my wife during these early years of my daughters' infancy, the walls stop growing, and my heart remains open to all the goodness we experience as a family.

7

GROWING UP WITH YOUR KIDS

John McMahon

Being an active, involved father is not easy. It's something you learn as you grow up with your kids.

There was never any doubt that my wife, Peg, and I were going to have kids, and that we were both going to take an active role in their upbringing. As a couple, we split the household chores, shared the cooking, and both worked outside our home. Getting pregnant was by mutual consent; for nine months we both waited anxiously for our names to change to Mom and Dad.

After our daughter Lally was born, I still went to work, cut some wood, and watered the garden—all things I had done before. Peg's life, on the other hand, changed drastically: she took care of the baby and held the ultimate responsibility of always being there to give whatever was needed. Certainly our relationship changed. At times I felt jealous and left out, yet Peg and I always knew that our new baby was our priority at that moment. Whatever difficulties we, as a couple, encountered could be resolved eventually; we saw our marriage as being for a long time. Still, I did not exactly feel like a father. Lally did not want me much in those early months. She would put up with me for a while, but she really wanted her mom. I carried her around in the evenings when Peg needed a break, but it was always back to mama for the real thing. I finally came to believe that this is the way it should be. Those who believe that a baby should be bottle-fed, or that mama should pump breast milk so that dad can be involved in feeding, are missing the point of shared responsibility.

Lally and I got to be good friends after a while. Eighteen months after her birth, Finnie was born. If there ever was a boy who could scream, kick, and make his presence felt, here was one of the best. After rehearsing my parental responsibilities with Lally for a year and a half, my fathering role now went into full production. Peg spent those early days keeping the lid on; it was I who had to remember where the pins were left.

While Peg excelled at her 2:00 a.m. singing routine with Finn, I deciphered Lally's nighttime squirms and grunts. I did spend some evenings with Finn as well. I was famous for my colic carry and had a friend in the squeaky rocking chair, but the nighttime fathering of a tiny baby was not my favorite pastime. Ultimately, I knew Peg would bail me out.

Things had just begun to calm down when, two and a half years after Finnie's arrival, Bram was born. My nighttime fathering skills were revived. No longer could I rely on Peg to get up with one of the kids, as she had her hands full with the baby. When she finally was able to rest, it did not seem fair for her to have to jump up because one of the older children awoke. It became an unwritten law that I would take care of them at night—drinks, bathroom trips, dreams, aches and pains.

I worked outside the home from the beginning of our marriage. As a result, the chores were not shared as much as they might have been. I had a couple of favorite meals I liked to cook once in a while, but Peg is a wonderful cook and did most of the cooking through the years. As a result, we got into the habit of her cooking and my doing the total cleanup, even to the last couple of disgusting pans. I now have very high standards for clean, spotless dishes, prefer certain cleaning products to others, and would never allow dirty dishes to sit in the sink overnight.

I think that the big step in any kind of sharing arrangement comes when you become absolutely responsible for a job, when no one is going to bail you out when things get a little hard. No one is going to do those last couple of dirty pans that you left soaking in the sink or fold the clothes you left on the dryer the night before. As Peg got busier with the babies, I started getting busier with the house. She could not keep up with the laundry, and I needed clean clothes for work. I soon discovered that everyone else in the family wore the same clothes all the time; I was the one who generated most of the laundry and ironing. One thing led to another, and I became intimately involved with lights and darks, cottons and rayons, shrinkables and non-shrinkables, hot and cold water. I do slide a little bit on the folding end. I save up the loads and only sort them when no more can be

JOHN SCHOENWALTER

piled on the dryer. It is always fun to have a folding party with the kids. Since I was the only one who needed it, the ironing became my job as well. It's still not my favorite thing to do, so I have turned into a morning ironer. (I always have a couple of backup shirts for those overslept days.)

I think that anyone who tries to establish a nonsexist environment for their children will find that as much as we try to be neutral, little girls and little boys are just plain different in many ways. However, one area where children of both sexes are the same is in their ability to take responsibility for helping around the house. If we take the attitude that housework is women's work, then we will be doing children a great disservice and cause problems for them later in life.

The other attitude to discard is one often held by men: namely, that you are somehow less of a man if you are involved with your children and the management of the house and place these things as the number one priority in your life. Hopefully this attitude is changing, as more and more men come out of this particular "closet" and share family responsibilities.

We all have different concepts of the perfect marriage or the perfect family. If you make a commitment to share in the raising of your children and to be an active father, then whatever it takes to get to that end is the best thing to do. It is a process that grows with time, with the coming of children and age. It is not easy, and the track record for marriages is not great. I think, though, that if your marriage is based on a commitment to share in the effort and is open enough to allow restructuring, then the odds for joy will be in your favor.

8

EARLY DAYS AS A STEPFATHER

David Morton

Jealousy! Resentment! Who'd have ever thought I could feel these emotions so strongly and toward such a little person! I just didn't want her around!

When Lisa and I first met, soon after her mother and I began seeing each other, we were quite friendly, but after a few weeks the situation started to deteriorate. My relationship with her mother quickly intensified, and jealousy reared its ugly head. I resented the fact that Judith gave her nine-year-old daughter so much of her time and attention, and Lisa was jealous of me because I took her mother's attention away from her.

The romance between Judith and me grew. After a few months, I moved in with her and her daughter. Unknowingly, I also stepped into an authoritarian role with Lisa. We argued regularly about minor things and usually pulled Judith into the arguments as well. Harmony seemed impossible. When summer came, Lisa flew to Ohio to visit her father and his family. While she was gone, I realized that I had expected our relationship to be father-to-daughter from the start. I enjoyed the time alone with Judith but became apprehensive when I thought about Lisa being with us again in the fall. Neither of us were meeting my expectations, and I did not look forward to her return.

In retrospect, I think our relationship was initially so difficult because we had not recognized the need to define our roles and responsibilities as members of a family. Lisa spoke of her father a lot in those early days, seemingly comparing him to me. I knew I could not take his place, but at the same time, I secretly hoped to be accepted as a dad.

When the three of us moved into a two-bedroom house after Lisa's return from Ohio, there was noticeably less tension. Having more elbow room gave each of us the space we needed to become more open to each other. If we weren't getting along, each of us now had a room to retreat to. Lisa and I now occasionally did things together without Judith. We had a great time going to the movies or out for ice cream. It was during these times that I actually started to get to know and like Lisa. She acted differently toward me, and I saw her as a real person, separate from Judith.

The three of us started having house meetings to verbalize and clarify the connection we shared. We would begin by sitting in a circle, holding hands, and meditating for a few minutes; then we'd talk about our feelings and future plans and voice any grievances we had. Judith and I stressed that truthfulness was very important. As Lisa and I shared our feelings with each other, our arguments often turned into discussions, with Judith occasionally acting as a nonbiased mediator. The three of us were learning to cooperate and learn from each other.

We developed a list of household chores we all agreed needed to be done, then chose the ones we each preferred to do. Sweeping, vacuuming, food preparation, dishes, laundry, taking out the trash, shopping, and cleaning the bathroom were all included. Lisa even opted for fixing dinner one night a week. She seemed to enjoy that responsibility, and I felt proud that a ten-year-old could fix dinner for three. It seemed that mutual cooperation was evolving.

Another summer blossomed, and Lisa was off on her annual expedition to Ohio. After she returned for the new school year, the first few weeks were torture. It appeared that the positive ground we had gained before her departure was lost. None of us got along, and we argued a lot. It was a difficult transition.

However, even in those trying times, there were moments of good feeling between Lisa and me. Some evenings we all played Scrabble or Yahtzee together; at other times we'd collaborate on a thousand-piece puzzle. Occasionally, the three of us would go to the beach, where Lisa and I enjoyed flying kites and beachcombing together. Sometimes we'd pack a picnic dinner and eat while we watched the sun set into the ocean. Those were happy times for us all.

Sad to say, those moments of positive interaction weren't enough to balance the negative times. Lisa and I started to argue more often. I wanted our difficulties to be resolved, but that became difficult. Judith and I started arguing more as well, usually disagreeing about the

way to handle difficult situations with Lisa. We felt the best thing for all of us was to separate, so I moved out.

After a few weeks apart, we all agreed to sit down together and try to work things out. Following a long, emotional discussion, we embraced in a loving three-way bear hug. We agreed on one major point: we all wanted to be together as a family. I moved back into the house, backing off from the father role and focusing on being Lisa's friend. Though we still had our frustrating moments, we put more conscious effort into resolving our problems. As time passed, we grew closer. Lisa started coming to me for help and assistance rather than going exclusively to Judith. It seemed that my prayers for acceptance were being answered, and I found that I was becoming more open as well.

Still, we all yearned for a deeper relationship with more commitment and fulfillment. After receiving counseling (we both had been married before), Judith and I decided to get married and publicly share our commitment as a family. Lisa was just as excited as Judith and I. She was not only beside us at the ceremony but was also an integral part of it. Judith and I pledged our love and support to each other as well as to the well-being of our family.

After the ceremony, Lisa and I became more loving toward each other. The open, verbal commitment of Judith's and my marriage vows seemed to strengthen our bond and make her feel more secure. I was no longer just Judith's boyfriend; I was now "related" to her. How my heart sang when she walked in from school and greeted me with open arms. She started referring to me as "dad" and "father," and I responded lovingly to my new "daughter." It was apparent that, in both of us, needs for family were becoming fulfilled. Our friendship grew, and so did our love.

After several years of being together, I can see that we all have made significant, positive changes. Instead of being the strict disciplinarian I used to be, I have become more patient and accepting of Lisa. I have begun to see her as a separate person as well as a daughter, which has created great possibilities for our relationship in the future. In the early days, I used threats and punishment in response to what I saw as Lisa's disobedience. In retrospect, I realize that some of those difficult situations arose from Lisa not meeting *my* expectations. In the past few months, we have changed the concept of "punishment" to a more positive concept of "consequences of actions," thus giving Lisa the responsibility for her behavior.

I have also learned that I receive a more positive response by sharing my thoughts and feelings with Lisa, rather than by saying, "You are this way," or "You did that," and, in effect, placing the responsibility for my reactions on her. Now I explain that "I think" and "I feel" her actions have affected me in a certain way, and she responds in a more conscious, caring manner. This process moves in a more positive direction, with more affirmative results.

I am now beginning to understand what "leaving something behind for our children" really means. If I can be more understanding and loving with Lisa, then she will, in turn, be more positive with others with whom she comes in contact. Our family is striving to make truth, love, and mutual respect a conscious part of our lives. It is a never-ending process.

9

The Litany of Childhood

Paul Michaels

In a few months, my daughter will be three. She is a joy, always full of laughter. Her little jokes fill the house. At least a dozen times a day, we recite a litany that goes like this:

"Knock, knock," she asks.

"Who's there?" I reply.

"Mickey Mouse's underwear!"

We both break into rounds of laughter. The joke seems new to her each time. It is beginning to seem new to me as well.

As fathers will, I worry about her: her health, her relationship with her mother and her brothers and sisters, going to school, her first love and first broken heart, her self-expression in the world, and even whether there will be a world for her when she grows up. She has been through a lot in her first years: her mother and father's estrangement and eventual separation; living in at least half a dozen places; and the many late-night arguments that characterize a dying relationship.

In spite of all this, she is truly a wonderful being. People stop us on the main street of the small town we live in and comment on her obvious élan vital. I look at her again and again, sleeping and awake, and find myself in agreement. She is beautiful.

I try to remember what it is like to be "almost" three. What were my thoughts and emotions? What did I do? Was I as joyful and full of life as she is? I think not. I was adopted and can remember only parts of my feelings and emotions. Mostly, I remember the aloneness. My adoptive parents provided a wonderful home with a nurturing environment. They truly loved me and still do. But the pain is there. I remember it.

Does my daughter have such pain? I notice she tells me very easily

when and why she is sad. She also tells me when and why she is
happy. I find myself admiring the ease with which she expresses herself. I wish I could have done the same at her age. I wish I could do the
same at my age!

Trying to remember my own childhood has brought with it the
unexpected bonus of an added richness in my relationship with my
daughter. Perhaps this comes from my attempts to link up with my
past? I don't know, for I really can't put my finger on it. But something
is happening. It is as if my trying to remember brings forth from
within me a childlike quality that allows us to communicate in new
and unexpected ways. Our shared humor may be an example of this
phenomenon.

Now she is standing beside me. "Daddy, let's go for a walk," she
says.

We begin our walk down Main Street. I soon disappear within
myself, thinking. "Daddy, talk to me," she scolds. This is also part of
our ritual.

So I begin to talk. We talk about her mommy and her brothers and
sisters and her latest drawing, about her next pizza and about what it
is like living together and taking baths together, and whether she
brought her vitamin C in her pocket (along with a few marbles, sugar-
less gum wrappers, and some of her pennies).

Again, I lapse into silence. I wonder whether our living together
most of the week is working out. She also spends a few days with her
mother. Am I willing to live with my daughter full-time? I think about
this.

We round the corner and begin the homeward part of our journey.
We approach the toy store, and I make a mental check of how much
money I have in my wallet. Do I have enough for a small toy? We both
like the little windup ones. They are especially fun in the bathtub.

She is now asking me whether we can go into the toy store. Has this
all been planned? If so, she has planned well. We go in.

As we continue our walk later, we come upon a pile of day-old ice
from the fish market. She loves playing with it. Having grown up in
California, she hasn't seen snow yet. I hold her new toy, one which we
both will enjoy. It's a biplane with a propeller that goes around when
pushed. I again find myself thinking about snow, about growing up in
the Midwest, about winters and sleds and hot cocoa and the excitement of the first snow of the winter. I find myself wanting to share

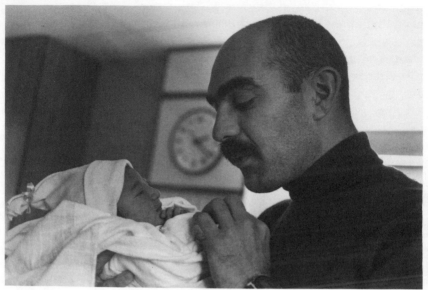

my memories with her. I try telling her about snow and snowmen, but she gives me only a perfunctory hearing. Her reality right now is the ice from the fish market. I lament that there isn't enough for a snowman.

We are now only a few blocks from home. Her hands are cold. She asks me to notice how cold her hands are. I tell her they are so cold they are making Daddy's hands cold. She thinks that must be pretty cold to make Daddy's hands cold.

Approaching the Masonic Temple, I notice that someone has cut all the beautiful wildflowers that grew on the sides of its driveway. Our walks had included talking about the flowers and taking a few home for our kitchen table. Now we will have to wait until next spring to pick flowers here again.

The last part of our walk home is uphill. I expect to be asked for a ride. But today there is a change in the litany. There is no request. Instead, we walk hand in hand up the small hill. I find myself trying to remember the last time my dad and I went for a walk. I can't. I do remember our early morning turtle searches along the country roads where I grew up, outings that were usually successful.

We are now on the downhill final half-block. My daughter runs ahead of me, showing me how fast she can run. As I watch, waiting for the appropriate moment to comment on her speed, I again think about her living with me full-time. It can work for me. I will need to make a few changes in my schedule. But will it work for her? I know she needs and loves her mother. She has told me that. She also told me yesterday she enjoys going back and forth between her mother and me.

I do not want her to lose her beauty, her élan. I suddenly have the feeling she won't. In spite of everything, she will more than survive. I know deep within that it really doesn't make a difference where she lives. She will make whatever situation she finds herself in work for her. She will surround herself with loving and caring people.

The walk is over now. We are inside, in separate parts of the house. She is probably drawing one of her many pictures. I am thinking again about her and our life together when suddenly she is beside me.

"Daddy," she intones.

"Yes," I reply.

"Knock, knock!"

"Who's there?"

"Mickey Mouse's underwear," comes the response, and we both break into peals of laughter.

10

A Matter of Enlightenment

Peter J. Dorsen

Being involved in the nurturing process is a constant source of self-revelation for many fathers. Lettie Pogrebin, in her books *Family Politics* and *Growing Up Free*, advocates "more dad and less mom" as well as a balance of power and love between partners.[1] She promotes a way of life that my wife, Susy, and I struggle to practice.

Sharron Humenick and Larry Bugen, in "Parenting Roles: Expectation vs. Reality," emphasize that despite the shift away from traditional definitions of male and female roles in child care, women usually end up providing more care than men and some partners harbor resentment toward each other.[2] Indications are that the nurturing father, although more desirable and common than he once was, is not easy to come by. As the proud father of three daughters, I can testify to the struggle. A professional with peer and family expectations to earn a living, I have been able to shift my priorities, but only after taking a hard look at those expectations and confronting the unspoken judgments of some of my colleagues, who question not whether I am finding meaning in life or spending enough time with my young children but whether I am earning enough money to support my family (preferably by working nine hours a day) and what my earning potential is.

Fathers and Babies

Pogrebin's study of how much time men spend with their children is alarming. The average father interacts with his baby less than thirty-eight seconds a day. When I first read those figures, what really made me squirm was that half of the three- to four-year-olds questioned preferred watching TV to spending time with their fathers. Fortunately, half the children interviewed wished their fathers would spend more time with them.[3] Time study completed, I biked right home and "interviewed" my oldest daughter. The only twist was that I asked if she preferred going swimming with me over watching TV. She went for the swim!

Pogrebin comments, "When playtime is measured, fathers may well equal or even surpass mothers." However, when caring time is measured, fathers are largely absent.[4] Could this mean that despite the increasing incidence of paternity leaves, many of us new dads are actually paying lip service to a father's importance in the nurturing process?

Humenick and Bugen, who found that most studies portray early parenting largely in terms of mothering, set out to explore the realities of fathering. They interviewed thirty-seven middle-class couples, with a mean age of twenty-five, attending Lamaze classes in a university community. They then compared prenatal expectations with the amount of time each parent actually spent in active involvement with the baby. The mothers ended up spending *more* time holding, feeding, changing, and touching than they had anticipated, while the fathers spent *less* time than expected on every item, especially in the areas of changing, touching, washing, playing, or talking. Only three of the thirty-seven fathers interviewed reported spending more time with their babies than they had expected.

The researchers were surprised to find this "branching effect" between parental expectations and involvement.[5] Could it be that in attempting to surmount the unfortunate stereotypes and expectations of traditional roles, we new fathers are overlooking the realities of parenting? If we share the power *and* the responsibilities, we will ultimately reap the joys of a happier marriage and a better relationship with our children.

Humenick and Bugen point out that "one factor influencing the amount of parental involvement with the infant is how much support the mother feels she is getting from the father." Conversely, it seems that "her help and encouragement would also tend to increase the amount of time her partner devotes to fathering," since she is likely to be his major, and often only, support in this role.[6]

The question is, just how much is either parent communicating his or her frustration with parenting responsibilities? How much problem solving is actually going on? A father who interacts minimally during his child's first few weeks may miss some of the important cues initiated by the child. Since approximately 50 percent of parent-child interactions during the first few weeks are initiated by the child,[7] the father who does not participate during this early stage may be slower to learn and respond to his infant's cues. So here we have a wife struggling to provide more infant care than she assumed was in the "prenatal agreement" and an equally frustrated father, disappointed because he has fewer initial responsibilities than expected and an unequal opportunity to bond with his child.

How to avoid this situation? The investigators suggest that couples learn to be more supportive of each other both before and after birth. They propose exploring simple questions, such as, "How do you think you would respond if you find that your wife is concerned about how much time it takes to care for the baby but you aren't spending as much time with the baby as you had hoped?" or "How would you respond if the baby takes more of your time than you thought and your husband is feeling left out?" They also suggest that new fathers gain exposure to the skills and peer support needed to increase confidence in their parenting roles.

I have little doubt that whatever it may take to improve communication between partners can lead to a more loving relationship and better parenting. When I left a traditional job as a practicing physician two years ago, I found it difficult to get support from my male friends. The fact that, with rare exceptions, I was the only man out in the parking lot at three in the afternoon to pick up my daughter at school did not reap praise from my male friends who were working eight to five. Moreover, the one father who spent even more time at the school than I did never returned after the first quarter, thus ending a certain kinship I felt toward him.

Laura Lein, in *Family Coordinator*, explains that "men's ambivalence to changes in the structure of home life reflects the multiple pressures on them as citizens, workers, and concerned family members." She adds, "Men's values concerning paid work and their sex-specific relationship to the paid labor force conflict with increased involvement in the day-to-day functioning of the home."[8] This was certainly true in my case. I will never forget the look of shock on the faces of my friends and colleagues when I quit practicing medicine to have more time with my family!

I explained to some that I was on maternity leave. For a year, I attempted to write in an office adjacent to our bedroom. I must con-

JOHN SCHOENWALTER

fess that ultimately I moved my word processor to an office, though not as much to decrease distractions as to set a limit on the amount of time I devoted to writing and thus increase my involvement with my family when I was home. I also like going to a work site, even though my income is not dependent on my presence there but rather on my productivity as a free-lancer. Maybe I needed some geographic distance between home and the workplace simply to be able to separate myself from my work.

Learning to Nurture

I grew up as an only child. Before I became a father, the closest I had ever come to nurturing a baby was during my pediatric rotation on the newborn ward in medical school. I recall feeling quite insecure examining the many fragile newborns for an appropriate number of toes and fingers, listening for heart murmurs, and performing standard neurological tests for their reflexes—not to mention changing diapers. Although my wife Susy grew up with a younger brother, she spent very little time baby-sitting. So, when we conceived our first child, neither she nor I thought to quantify how much time we would devote to parenting. What helped us adjust to the realities was the fact

that I left my job for a week after the birth (and changed every diaper).
I awoke whenever Bria did and usually transported her from her
bassinet to Susy's breast. Carrying my daughter everywhere, in my
arms or in the Snugli, was an important chance for me to bond with
our new family member as well as an essential opportunity for Susy to
recover from labor.

However, once the week was over, so, too, was the "honeymoon."
Once back at work, I found it harder to awake at night. It would
sometimes take a blowup between Susy and myself to remind me that
I had slipped back into a traditional role. "Mother providing child
care and father working only eight to five" was clearly not what I
wanted for my family, so I began to take on more of the evening nurturing. It became my role to help with dinner, clean up, play with
Bria, bathe her, ready her for bed, and read a bedtime story—usually
in a rocking chair.

A public health nurse who paid us a routine visit after Bria was
born found Susy and me sitting out on the lawn enjoying some sun.
Bria, propped against a birch tree, slept peacefully in the shade. We
were reassured to learn that our relaxed parenting style was OK, and
we were eager to ask questions. We wanted information not only on
the nitty-gritty matters, such as how to care for the umbilical cord,
but also on ways to demystify roles traditionally reserved for the
woman. We were both involved in child care, and we wanted to keep
it that way.

We are now nurturing three children. Just as our love has expanded
to encompass each addition to our life, we have found that we must
expand our openness to new roles. Breast-feeding has solidified the
early relationship Susy develops with each child. For me, early bonding has been strengthened by countless walks with my baby nestled in
a Snugli against my chest. The hundreds of baths I have shared, first
with one child and then another, have provided a joyous intimacy
and a special domain for me and my children. And singing songs like
"Irene, Good Night" has drawn me close to my daughters.

What has helped Susy and me remain open to new roles is the support we offer each other for jobs well done. I have learned to fully
appreciate my wife's day-to-day challenges. I have also learned that
keeping a clean house with young children is like "shoveling the walk
before it stops snowing."9 And Susy's compliments for what I do make
all the difference in my feelings of self-worth as a parent. How good

it feels to hear her say, "You really handled Bria's frustration calmly," or "I appreciate that you took the kids swimming so I could get some rest." This kind of praise does not come from anyone else.

We also make a point to keep communicating about our parenting roles. As our children and our family grow, needs change and priorities shift, and it is easy to feel that one or the other of us is not getting a fair deal. After one discussion, I agreed to replace Susy in a parenting group that is now composed of thirteen mothers and me! I feel honored to be included and often joke that I am bound to learn new techniques to bring to my men's group. Susy and I update our communication regularly during our one night out a week. This is our special time for enjoying an uninterrupted meal and open conversation. Frustrations melt away as we relax and remember what it was that brought us together in the first place.

For me, a loving relationship with my partner has generated involved fathering, and parenting itself has shown me the way to be a better parent. Even after a busy day with my girls, I look forward to being with them as they drift off to sleep. I stroke their hair, kiss them, and tell them how much their father loves them.

Notes

1. Lettie Pogrebin, *Family Politics* (New York: McGraw-Hill, 1983) and *Growing Up Free* (New York: McGraw-Hill, 1980).
2. Sharron S. Humenick and Larry A. Bugen, "Parenting Roles: Expectation vs. Reality," *Maternal Child Nursing* 12 (Jan./Feb. 1987): 36-39.
3. Lettie Pogrebin, *Growing Up Free*, 142.
4. Lettie Pogrebin, *Family Politics*, 202.
5. See n. 2.
6. Ibid.
7. Ibid.
8. Laura Lein, "Male Participation in Home Life: Impact of Social Supports and Breadwinner Responsibility on the Allocation of Tasks," *Family Coordinator* (Oct. 1979): 489.
9. Phyllis Diller, "Housekeeping Hints," reprinted in *Family Politics*, 42.

11

BEING BABA

Joseph Polselli

Nine and a half months after her birth, Mikaela smiled at me from across the room and took twelve teetering steps into my arms. For the next three weeks, I bored everyone who came near me with my account of what had happened. But after all, those were the first steps she had ever taken. Any father can understand how I felt as I lifted her triumphantly overhead and saw scuff marks on the bottoms of her tiny slippers.

Like me, Mikaela's parents, Randi and Jim, had cheered with lumps in their throats. I have known them for sixteen years, during which time our friendship has grown into an extraordinary partnership. In fact, my alliance with Jim and Randi is as important to them as the intimate conjugal bond they share with each other. This doesn't get kinky. We don't have a sexual triangle, and we have no interest in starting a new religion. What we do have is as practical as it is uncomplicated: a mature relationship based on goodwill, compatibility, a give-and-take attitude, and common goals. Our high regard for one another extended naturally to Mikaela, so she entered the world with not two but *three* loving adults to help her thrive.

A history of shared experiences and unusual approaches to life's challenges has led to our co-parentage of Mikaela. For almost as long as we've known one another, all of our resources, including money, have been pooled. Several years ago, in an effort to trim our budgets and build up some savings, the three of us tent-camped through a fierce New Hampshire winter. Soon thereafter, we pedaled our bicycles across much of America. It wasn't just a pleasure trip. We were moving as economically as possible from New Hampshire to California, and our bicycles were the moving vans.

We built homes for one another on our shared mountain property, carrying every brick, beam, and board up the three-quarter-mile climb to our house sites. When Jim and Randi were married in our orchard, I didn't simply attend their wedding, I wrote the ceremony. (As their best man, it took me three tries and a soggy napkin to get through the toast.) It was this kind of closeness that brought us together in the local clinic's birthing room in 1983 and motivated Jim and Randi's decision to inform me that the child whose birth we awaited was not so much theirs as *ours*.

We waited all night for Mikaela to come. I held the flashlight and watched the crown of her head inch toward me and slip ever so slightly back again. Randi eventually located her evasive "pushing" muscles by pressing one foot against her midwife's thigh, while Jim touched the palm of his hand against her lower back and whispered encouragement.

Mikaela arrived at dawn. When her head slipped out it swiveled from side to side, and her eyes made contact with Jim's and mine. Her entry into the world was gentle, and our tears anointed her. Mikaela fit so perfectly in the crook of Randi's arm that it was as if nature had measured and shaped them to each another.

Jim and I shared our own special bond. In relation to this newborn child, we were of one mind and one feeling. He had become a father, and we both knew that I had become a father, too.

Despite the rarity of such friendships in modern times, my relationship with Jim, Randi, and Mikaela is not without precedent. In fact, the concept of co-parenthood has existed since the time of the early Greeks. By the fifteenth century, it had evolved into a practice of the Roman Catholic Church wherein godparents and parents shared the responsibility for the child's material and spiritual needs. In every practical sense, a godparent was the equal of a blood relative.

In their classic analysis of ritual co-parenthood, "An Analysis of Ritual Co-Parenthood (Compadrazgo)" (*Southwestern Journal of Anthropology* 6 [1950]: 360), Sidney Mintz and Eric Wolf report that a hapless fifteenth-century man named John Howthon "was whipped three times around the market and church for having married a girl to whom his first wife had been godmother." By today's standards, John Howthon's choice of mate might raise an old-fashioned eyebrow but would hardly be considered incestuous; yet such was the seriousness with which co-parent relationships once were entered into.

In much of the world today, choosing godparents is largely a formal practice void of meaning. A godparent or co-parent is no longer expected to adopt the child in the event of the parent's death or provide for the child while the parents still live. So, in important ways, the kinship we enjoy revives some venerable and pragmatic customs.

The godparent model, however, supplied no answer to the question of what Mikaela should call me. I wasn't quite her godfather, at least not in today's sense of the term. She had started by calling me "Dada," but that was society's name for Jim's role and, in a biological sense, did not precisely describe me. We considered "Uncle Joey," but felt that we'd be borrowing a category (uncle) that named another kind of relationship. It was during a recent tour of India that I happened upon the Hindi word *Babuji*, or father. It had the advantage of sounding different from "Dada" while retaining the same meaning. Mikaela approved at once. She shortened it to "Baba" and has used it ever since.

In addition to having a "Baba," Mikaela has another unique aspect to her life. The mountain home we jointly fashioned provides her with limitless opportunities. Ever since her birth day in the clinic, her life has been lived mostly outdoors. With the exception of winter, when she is inside their cabin, she sleeps alongside Jim and Randi on our observation tower, with open views to the mountains, the stars, and her favorite celestial body of all, the moon.

Throughout the mild weather, which lasts for six months here, she lives and plays with us in an outdoor kitchen and recreation area that we fashioned out of recycled lumber from an abandoned mill. Her playpen has no bars; it is an open field of clover, wildflowers, and fruit trees, bordered on every side by giant conifers. The diverse plants, insects, and animals endlessly fascinate her, and she is always eager to show us what she has found. Having three parents increases the possibility that at least one of us will be free to share in the excitement of a mouse nest in the woodpile or a newborn fawn crouching behind the fallen cedar.

Perhaps her unusual exposure to such wonders stimulated her curiosity and helped trigger her early venture into language. With three adults to converse with and learn from, Mikaela has had many opportunities to communicate her enthusiasm about the world. At only fifteen months, she was able to speak in sentences and would sometimes identify an object whose name none of us could remember having taught her. On her own initiative, she would often string

JILL FINEBERG

words together to convey her sentiments. "Thanks for the presents, Baba," became her way of showing appreciation for the stories we read and the games we played together.

Crawling and then walking the uneven forest floor has undoubtedly accelerated the development of her climbing skills. At fourteen months, she had conquered without assistance the steep, three-quarter-mile trail to our cabins. It seems only last week that she took those twelve uncertain steps into my arms.

Sharing parental responsibility with Jim and Randi means an equal voice for each of us in decisions affecting Mikaela—how we relate to her, how we reward her, and how we deal with unreasonable demands. Because we implicitly trust one another, we are usually quick to achieve a consensus. In truth, we are even closer because of our love for her, a love that guides every decision we make in her regard.

One of the most rewarding aspects of this adventure has been Mikaela's openness to it. Having come into the world with no preconceptions, she accepts her expanded nuclear family without qualification. One of her favorite pastimes is to play in the field while reciting our names as if they were one reassuring word: "Daddymommy-

babamommybabadaddy." Last summer, when Randi, without fore-
thought, identified three lizards as a mama, papa, and baby, Mikaela
would not rest until she had completed the family, to her satisfaction,
by finding a "baba" lizard nearby.

I never realized that fatherhood could be so good. I know that if I
one day become the biological father of a child, I will love that child
as much as I love Mikaela—no more and no less. As adoptive parents
can attest, the parents of a child are those involved in raising him or
her and the love that adoptive parents feel for their child is as
unqualified and complete as the love of biological parents. Mikaela's
case, however, is unique; she has added one adoptive parent while
maintaining her two originals.

Being Baba is a comfortable niche for me. I am able to devote a por-
tion of my time to my writing career while still enjoying the warmth
and intensity that family life brings. My unique relationship to
their daughter opens up possibilities for Jim and Randi, too. Jim can
work away from home sometimes, assured that his family is well cared
for, while Randi can find time occasionally for her studies in botany,
knowing that one of Mikaela's two "fathers" will be there to look after
her. The entire situation makes for three happy parents, which goes a
long way toward creating a stimulating world for the baby.

The four of us have seen a lot together, and we're optimistic about
the future. Mikaela has the secure environment she needs, and this
should pave the way for healthy independence later on. Yet whatever
help we give her now can barely compensate for the joy and love that
she has already given to us. Thanks for the presents, Mikaela.

12

PARABLE

Don Richmond

There was once a devout man who lived in a small house with his wife. They led a good life, working hard and trying to be virtuous. Sometimes this man was quite happy, but more often his heart was torn by feelings of longing and incompletion. He yearned to be completely open and loving to all, to cast aside his selfishness and limitations and to be a holy man. Many times he asked the Lord for a sign or for a teacher to show him the way.

One day as he was working, the man saw his wife running toward him. "Come quickly," she cried. "Something has happened to fill our lives with happiness!" Hurrying back to their house, the man was silent but filled with expectations. Perhaps, finally, someone or something had come to teach and help him.

The woman pulled him by the sleeve through the door of their small home and pointed at a large basket on the table. "A boy-child, left on our doorstep!" she exulted. "The Lord sent him to us, since we have no children of our own." The man looked warmly at the baby, for he loved children and had often wanted a son. However, he could not help feeling a little disappointed as he thought, "What can a baby who knows nothing show me?"

The boy was a beautiful child, open and clear. He showed his true heart always, as babies will. The man did his work and watched the boy grow. He treated him kindly, though his heart was not always fully in it. Part of him was still somewhere else, looking and searching for completion.

The man often liked to spend time walking in the forest, admiring nature. One day, on such a walk, he sat down on a rock, marveling at the overwhelming quiet and calm that surrounded him, and felt himself becoming still and peaceful like the forest. He smiled as thoughts

and images from his life, particularly of his wife and son rose in his
mind. "Yes, this has been my life. I accept it. It has not been a bad
one."

Sitting there, he remembered two old sayings. One was: "Seek and
you shall find." Another was: "Only he who loses his life in service to
others shall truly find it." These words turned themselves over in
his mind, weaving themselves into the tapestry of his life, and he realized in a flash what was being revealed to him. As a blind man
restored to sight, he saw that the baby that had come to him had
shown him a love, an openness, and a vision of the higher, clearer
part of existence that he had not seen before. With this, he saw the
great opportunity for service that the baby had brought him. The one
thought in his mind now was to rush back to his house and pour out
his love to his son, to do things for him, to guide him, and to enjoy him.

But when he reached home, the baby was gone. In his place stood a
young man full of the fire of youth. He believed himself stronger and
smarter than his father: he did not want the love or tenderness of a
sentimental old man.

The man was downcast, but his love for his son poured out of him
anyway. Cleansed, opened, and purged of selfishness, he saw beauty

and goodness everywhere, in his life and in his son's. He realized now that he must show his love for his son by letting him go his own way; by letting him blunder and fall if he must in order to learn, just as the man himself had done in scorning help and advice and in always searching for perfection. He knew now that though he wanted to guide and protect his child, to let him go his own way and learn for himself the great laws of life was the greatest sacrifice and the greatest love.

Even as the man had asked, so had he received. His answer and his goal had been there with him all the time, only requiring his acceptance to reveal their presence.

13

LOVE, FATHER

Posy Gering

Once, there was a father who had a son whom he loved very much. But when the boy was sixteen, he ran away from home.

He didn't tell anyone where he had gone. Nobody heard from him for many years. Finally, the son wrote his father and told him where he was living.

The father immediately wrote, saying, "Come back. Come home."

The son wrote back, "I can't. I can't come back."

The father replied, "Well, come back as far as you can, and I will meet you there."

PART III:
FATHERS AND WORK

14

BALANCING FATHERHOOD AND CAREER

John Byrne Barry

You can hardly flip through a magazine these days without coming across a story about a mother balancing career and family. And it only takes a spin or two of the channel selector to catch another TV report on the crisis in child care caused by the increasing numbers of women in the work force. Where are the daddies in these stories? Do they just mail in their chromosomes between business meetings? Aren't there any fathers rushing from the changing table to the conference room with diaper wipes streaming from their pockets?

We *are* out here! We may be a demographic molehill, but a growing number of fathers are doing more than "pitching in." We are putting parenting ahead of career and sharing the burdens and joys of child care and housework.

It is not news that fathering has changed over the past generation or two, or that today's father is more involved in child care than his father was. Over 80 percent of fathers are now present in the delivery room when their children are born, and the days of dads never changing diapers are mostly behind us. We now know that real men can be caring dads.

But although the involved and nurturing father is becoming more visible and accepted, he is still generally regarded as a helper in the world of child care and housekeeping. He pitches in. He helps *when he wants to.* Fathers are volunteer providers; mothers are the staff. The household with two "staff parents" is still rare, especially when such an arrangement requires the father to cut back on work.

TV commercials show fathers in business suits ducking out of conferences to attend their children's school plays, but we do not see them ducking out of work for the plain-old-vanilla caretaking of their children—the "quantity time" stuff. Support for father involvement in quantity time is growing in the work world with the speed of a glacier. Whereas employers may not allow a mother to work part-time, they do understand her reason for wanting to. However, a man who wants to work part-time in order to care for his children is looked on with suspicion or, at best, amusement.

Hollywood films, considered by some to be harbingers of popular culture trends, also present the notion that it's OK to be a dad as long as it's temporary. Movies such as *Three Men and a Baby* and *Mr. Mom* depict men who have child-care duties thrust upon them. These fathers learn to cope with and even thrive on parenting, but in the end they are "rescued" by mom taking over the primary caretaker role so dad can fade into the background. The implication here is that Dad is OK as a pinch-hitter, but he just doesn't have the stamina or desire for the long haul. His role is to be out earning money.

Sharing Child Care

My wife Laurie and I decided to share child care before our son Sean was even the proverbial twinkle in my eye. From the beginning, we strove for a relationship based on equality, and we divvied up the household chores with only occasional squabbles. But parenting is more than a chore; it's a life-style. Cognizant that our partnership could become unbalanced once a baby came squealing into the world, we deliberated carefully about how we'd manage the juggling act ahead.

Neither of us wanted to stop working, nor did we want to miss out on this exciting period of newborn growth by being the full-time bringer-home-of-bacon. As our childbirth educator said, "Your job will be there later, your friends will be there later, your hobbies will be there later, but your baby will never be a baby again." Besides, when was the last time you heard a man on his deathbed say, "I wish I had spent more time at work?"

In the months before our son was born, we both went to our employers and negotiated a reduction in working hours. We were able to juggle our time away from home so one of us could always be the primary caregiver. Fortunately, our employers were supportive, allowing us the flexibility to work at home and not balking at our patchwork schedules.

So, after the birth, I worked long hours two days a week while Laurie stayed home with Sean. On Tuesdays, I was home on the range. On Wednesdays and Fridays, we each worked a half day and spent the other half with Sean.

Fortunately, many variables came together for us. Because we both worked close to home—our commute time plus some overlap amounted to less than half an hour—we were able to manage half days. Laurie was also able to come home to breast-feed until Sean stopped nursing at fifteen months. And because I was already doing some of my writing and design work at home before Sean was born, it was fairly simple to formalize five hours of at-home work into my schedule. In addition, we both took the baby to work on occasion, mostly to pick up messages or drop things off. However, only in the first few months, when Sean's chief activity was sleeping, were we able to accomplish any real work with him in tow.

We managed this arrangement for seventeen months and then suffered a temporary setback. A restructuring at my workplace and a promotion I never asked for sent me across the bay to San Francisco, full-time. Despite an impassioned speech about why I should maintain a flexible schedule, I found myself a commuter dad, away from home eleven hours a day, five days a week. Laurie worked out shared baby-sitting agreements with two other mothers and called on her own mother to baby-sit once a week. Some weeks these arrangements worked, some weeks they didn't

The changes in my work schedule provoked changes in Sean. He began clinging more to his mother, and on the one evening a week that I soloed, he would wander through the house baaing "Mama" like a lost sheep, staying awake until she returned around 10:00 p.m.

After four months of full-time work—and a lot of grumbling—I found a flexible, 80-percent-time job as a publications coordinator. As the personnel manager put it, "This company supports the principle that a person can be professional and still work part-time." Although our situation is tighter and less flexible than it was originally, we have recovered our sense of balance. My relationship with Sean has improved dramatically.

We've been lucky, yes, but the determining factor for our success has been asking for and looking for suitable work arrangements. Requests for flexible scheduling are unlikely to be considered unless there is a demand for it. Although part-time professional work, job sharing, and working-at-home situations are still scarce, they have nevertheless entered the working world's vocabulary. According to

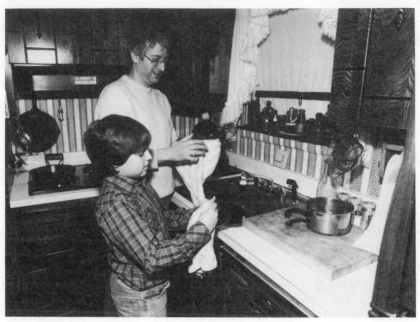

proponents of alternative work arrangements, such as the San
Francisco-based organization New Ways to Work, the most successful
route to a flexible situation is to create it yourself, and our experiences
attest to that. For now, this is more easily accomplished by workers
who have already established the trust and respect of their employers.

Our shared arrangement works well for the entire family. Sean is a
good-natured, energetic, outgoing, and secure child who laughs more
than he cries. When we are all at home, he sometimes wants his
mama and not me; but when Laurie is away, Sean and I have a great
time together. This phenomenon is borne out by the work of psychologist Diane Ehrensaft, who finds that in "soloing," fathers fare best,
because mothers are not around to invite comparisons.[1]

Sean's not the only one who is thriving. Laurie loves the balance of
playing with the baby and taking him for walks in the mornings and
then working on licensing contracts in the afternoons. And when
people at work ask where the baby is, she feels good saying, "He's with
his father." I also enjoy balancing the intellectual demands of work
with the emotional demands of parenting. The slower pace of my
hours with Sean gives me a fresh perspective on the worried, hurried
time frame of the working environment. The amount of time we

spend together frees us from having to have an agenda. We hang out, take aimless walks, play on the swings, eat ice cream, or sit on the corner and watch cars and trucks go by—one of Sean's favorite activities.

Although Laurie and I continue to strive toward equality in our parenting, we realize that it has never been *truly* equal—partly because Laurie logs more hours with Sean, but mostly because of the strong biological attachment between mother and child. Among couples who are committed to true equality in child care, mothers tend to nurse for just a few months or not at all.[2] For us, the importance of breast-feeding took precedence over any ideological commitment. In the early months, when Sean nursed a lot, our division of duties was weighted toward me doing most of the household stuff and Laurie doing most of the baby stuff. As Sean grew older and began to nurse less, we adjusted our division of labor. We seem to be mirroring what Kyle Pruett, M.D., calls the Jack Sprat theory of parenting: our contributions are not similar, but rather complementary.[3]

One way we keep current is by having "business meetings" on Friday evenings after Sean has gone to bed. This gives us a built-in opportunity to check in on how we are doing with our responsibilities as well as to synchronize calendars, schedule child care, balance checking accounts, and so on.

The Trade-offs

It is not all milk and honey, of course. Quantity time with Sean translates into a shortage of quantity time for his parents—for romance, for play, for sleep, and for keeping our living room from looking like the "before" picture in a miracle cleaner ad. We've also made sacrifices, but with our eyes wide open. We're renting a house instead of buying one. Career advancement is on idle. And although I know in my heart that nurturing a strong family is more important than having a deed on a house or a fat paycheck and an important title, it's tough to ignore all the people cruising by me on the fast track.

The careerism of the eighties and its squeezed-down timetable buzz like a mosquito in my ear. Not to have achieved a certain rung of success by the age of thirty-five is perceived as a failure. But what's the hurry? Here we are living longer than any preceding generation, and yet our collective energies are tied up in having it all *now*. I certainly hope to have it all, but in my lifetime, not in a week.

Actually, the career pressure has been of less concern than the lack of peers making similar choices. One of the questioning voices in my head has nagged, "If it's so right, how come more fathers aren't doing it?" I have often felt isolated as a father, a daddy lost in mommyland, especially on weekdays, when I find myself in a gym or on a playground filled with babies and their mothers.

Occasionally, when I'm tired and the dishes are piled high, or when Sean is hanging onto my pants as I scoop cottage cheese into a bowl for him, I think: "I'm doing what, a generation ago, my wife would have done without complaint. What if I had been born in an earlier era and Laurie were a more traditional wife and mother? Instead of changing Sean's diaper and feeding him and holding him when he's upset, I'd just bop in for some 'I'm gonna get yous,' roll around on the floor, and then head down to the bowling alley with the guys."
And be a full-time provider. *And* have less in common with my wife. *And* have to improve my bowling.

The "Mr. Mom" portrait of men as fathers—bathrobed, humiliated house-husbands sulking behind their vacuum cleaners while mom cuts multimillion dollar deals in her dress-for-success costume—is way off the mark. Men should feel good about taking care of children. The problem is that the work is devalued. Any mother knows that; it comes with the territory. But men are not used to walking these roads.[4]

When Sean was younger, one of my recurrent concerns was receiving the recognition I felt I deserved. I was waiting for the Congressional Medal of Honor to arrive in the mail, or my picture to appear on the cover of *Time* magazine, all for doing half as much as Laurie; for doing part-time for a year what millions of mothers do full-time for twenty years. What I did not realize at the time was that *every* engaged parent deserves recognition and that, as a man, I needed to unlearn the reward mentality of work.

Ehrensaft notes that men *have* been getting attention recently for their parenting. "We know full well that with all the recognition given to babies on men's laps and the visibility of fathers and children on Sunday strolls, the percentage of men and women who genuinely share the tasks of parenting is quite small. But the fact that such a practice is increasingly lauded rather than condemned is a large victory, one that will make it decidedly easier to receive social support for this new family style."[5]

She also notes that much of the renewed interest in flextime, on-site child care, and parental leave is due more to men's increased role in child care than to additional women in the work force. "Women have been in the work force for a long time. It is only recently that the influx of career men into involved fathering has occurred. As the attention has zoomed in on men involved with their children and as men have made more noises concerning its effects on their work and family lives, so American industry and government have given increased attention to the needs of working 'parents.' As in many other spheres, only when the more powerful male gender is affected is a social problem given public recognition."[6]

Both my need for recognition and my feelings of isolation have faded as Sean has grown older. So, too, have the voices in my head that challenge our decision to share child care. Sean, in his wonderful, preverbal way, tells me to listen to that deep-down-inside feeling that wants to be a daddy first and a guy with a job second. An ambassador of delight, he points his little fingers at strangers, cars, sunflowers, and dogs, babbling and giggling and infecting me with his joie de vivre.

When I was a child, no boy ever said he wanted to grow up to be a father. Hopefully, that is changing. Perhaps when Sean and other boys of his generation start thinking about what they want to be, some will say they want to be fathers. And perhaps, if and when they do become fathers and ask their employers for a reduced schedule in order to care for their children, they will be met with a knowing smile. Perhaps some of them will be the employers with the knowing smile.

Hopefully, by then, we will be further into what Betty Friedan calls the "second stage of feminism"—a time when men assume a larger role in child care, when men's desires for self-fulfillment beyond their jobs meet women's struggles for a life outside the home, and when these two forces combine to achieve an equitable balance between the sexes and between work and home responsibilities.[7] By then, society will hopefully have learned to support these new roles. We will know we have made it when *Gentlemen's Quarterly* starts featuring models with diaper pins as tie clasps.

Notes

1. Diane Ehrensaft, *Parenting Together: Men and Women Sharing the Care of Their Children* (New York: Free Press, 1987), 75.

2. Ibid., 45.

3. Kyle Pruett, M.D., *The Nurturing Father: Journey Toward the Complete Man* (New York: Warner Books, 1987).

4. James A. Levine, writing over twelve years ago in *Who Will Raise the Children? New Options for Fathers (and Mothers)* (Philadelphia: Lippincott, 1976), describes the doubt, skepticism, and rejection that a man can encounter when he takes on some of what has been traditionally viewed as female responsibility: "A nontraditional family structure presents *by its very existence* a questioning of the norm, and evokes strong feelings." (Italics mine.)

5. See n. 1, 252.

6. See n. 1, 260.

7. Betty Friedan, *The Second Stage* (New York: Summit Books, 1981).

For More Information

Literature

Cosby, Bill. *Fatherhood.* New York: Simon and Schuster, 1986.

Ehrensaft, Diane. *Parenting Together: Men and Women Sharing the Care of Their Children.* New York: Free Press, 1987.

Levine, James A. *Who Will Raise the Children? New Options for Fathers (and Mothers).* Philadelphia: Lippincott, 1976.

New Families Magazine: A Journal of Transitions. This quarterly addresses new work options and is available by subscription ($15.00 for one year) from NextStep Publications, 6340 34th Street SW, Seattle, WA 98126.

Pruett, Kyle, M.D. *The Nurturing Father: Journey Toward the Complete Man.* New York: Warner Books, 1987.

Organizations

New Ways To Work
149 Ninth Street
San Francisco, CA 94103
Offers public education, advocacy, and publications. Write for a complete listing of services and literature.

15

WEATHERING THE STORM TOGETHER

Howard Skeffington

I am a father who struggles a great deal with how to spend time with my family. Fatherhood has struck me right to the heart. Unfortunately, my job leaves me little room for flexibility. Frequent travel, unanticipated overtime, and weekend work occur all too often. Because of these threats to my familial existence, I make the most of my time with my wife and two children.

Let me tell you right up front that I am not a child psychologist, writer of children's books, pediatrician, or sociologist. But I am a dad. And as a dad, I must constantly face threats to my role as a nurturing, caring, participating member of the family. I think about my family every moment I am at work. It really tears at my soul to sit at a meeting away from home, knowing it will be hours before I see my son and daughter again. And I am not alone. I read that some 70 percent of men at work have a sense of guilt about leaving their children to the care of someone else.

But to me, the solution is not found in institutions like day-care centers, which, though they may fill society's economic needs, often broaden the chasm between the working parent and the child. In my life, the solution (or at least a beginning of the solution) is found by taking action where I have the most control: by not consuming my nonworking time with distractions.

Our modern, materialistic society is as cruel to the man whose fatherhood plays an integral role in his well-being as it is to the woman whose motherhood must compete with apparently conflicting individual goals and aspirations. There is no shortage of distractions to keep me from my desired fathering goals. This is perhaps more true today than at any other time in history, primarily due to the many at-home entertainment options, such as music, TV, and video, offered

MICHAEL WEISBROT

by the electronic media. Even when fathers are at home, they and their children may be glued to the TV rather than to each other. But the problem extends beyond the distractions themselves to a modern preoccupation with self-gratification and a form of individualism that leaves no room for family and, by extension, community. Little analysis is required to recognize that such preoccupation with self strains the family, and the family's decline saps the vitality of society.

The family is like a theater company of diverse personalities working toward a performance. None of the actors or stagehands can pull off a production alone: each person's unique contribution helps create something greater. The entire troupe suffers when the light technician decides to go out for coffee rather than execute light cues. The players play in the dark, and even the most magnificent script flops. Similarly, there's a negative effect on my family when I become engrossed in my golf game and forget that my family's goals also require my energies. Our common goals cannot be met this way. To realize family goals, I must be an active participant in my family and not just an income-generating figure in the background.

Now, I typically work an eight-hour day. I cannot afford to return home and expend what energy I have left on trivialities that do not contribute to the psychological care and feeding of my family. If

I enjoy watching television—and I do—I can postpone that habit until after my children are asleep. The same reasoning applies to participation in clubs and other outside activities that do not include the entire family. Since when does "socializing" mean "no children"? What do I really sacrifice by giving up a few distractions, as opposed to pursuing them at the expense of my family? I do not want to find out, when my children are teenagers, that I had confused priorities while they were young children.

I am not sure I have a consummate point to make. But I find myself often wondering just what it is that plagues American society. Why does there seem to be so much tension in the air? Why the high divorce rate? Why do the children of recent generations seem to be struggling more than those of previous generations? Why is crime on the rise from coast to coast? Why do we increasingly place the responsibility of raising our children on institutions? How do we find the roots of these problems and rip them from the soil? Why do I simply love my children's laughter and my wife's smile?

The difficulties associated with fathering in a world where measures of fulfillment and success focus on money, pleasure, and self cannot be overstated. The harvest reaped by my sacrificing a little time, maybe even a little sleep, hardly enhances my social stature at work. But the opportunity to nurture the bond between my wife and me and my children and me is a one-shot deal. I prefer to weather the storm of life *with* them.

16

WORKING FROM HOME

Charles Fletcher

Working at home with my wife has been a dream of mine for a long time. It started in 1983 when, as newlyweds, we managed a bed and breakfast inn together on the north coast of Oregon. The job lasted only ten months, and we were working for someone else, but the experience changed our lives profoundly. Ever since, we have tried hard to recapture that dream. In 1989, after six years of hard work, we succeeded, and returned to the north Oregon coast with our own desktop publishing business.

While managing the inn, I made a lot of discoveries about myself. Most important, I found that I loved working with Jan. Oh sure, we had disagreements and shouting matches over various things, but in general I found that I liked being with her throughout the day. Working together provided me with essential time to work on my relationship with her and to clear out the deadwood from my past. I felt that I had turned my feelings back on, after years of splitting my true self off from what I thought I had to do.

We left the inn when Jan became pregnant and returned to Seattle with hardly more than the shirts on our backs, a baby on the way, and a powerful dream: to one day start a home business and get back to that closeness we had experienced. Meanwhile, I had much soul-searching to do about what kind of parent I wanted to be. I had been a day-care kid in the 1950s and a latchkey kid (before there ever was such a term) after that. My father had been so mentally abused as a child by his father that, in order not to pass his sickness on to me, he cut himself off from me completely.

I didn't understand his motives at the time, and his neglect just made me crazy in a different way. My many experiences of loneliness, neglect, and general unhappiness as a child led me to give Jan as much support as I possibly could for being a stay-at-home mom. If I could have started a home business right then I would have, but I had no idea how to do it. I didn't know what type of business I wanted and was also pretty sure that I didn't have the money to get anything going, either.

The only thing that kept us going during those bleak times was our family, and our love for that happy little baby living in our midst. Jan sold toys in people's homes and made quilts and other handmade items to sell in crafts shows in an effort to continue to stay with our new child. Both of these activities were very unrewarding monetarily, but at the time we reasoned that we would spend more money on day-care, clothes, and transportation if she were to return to the traditional work force.

In hindsight, I can say that these first attempts at home business were more than dabbling; they were learning experiences. Not only did we learn that the crafts business was not for us, but we gained some knowledge about business licensing, what types of activities would be profitable, and most important, the necessity of choosing work that we loved to do. We also confirmed for ourselves that the only way we would succeed in our plan would be for Jan to work at home while raising our family. I would bring in a stable income until our as-yet-unborn home business grew enough for me to join it.

Many times in my first year of parenthood, I questioned this decision, especially when our financial troubles reached a feverish pitch. At the end of 1984, after inching along the razor's edge of financial disaster for a whole year, I went to the only employer who welcomed me with open arms, the only one who offered me a living wage: the army.

Joining the army was not a simple decision. It addressed not only our financial concerns but also the problems I'd had years earlier with my father. Since he'd ignored me for most of my life, I had never learned positive ways to experience life in the company of men. My mother was my main example for everything. My father didn't drive, he didn't play ball or any other games, he didn't fix things around the house. He was either at work or at home reading by himself most of the time. I learned all my basic life skills from my mother, and I'd always felt that I'd missed out somewhere in learning to be a man. As a result, the "manly" soldier skills that I could experience in the army seemed attractive to me when I enlisted.

At thirty-one, I was too old to join as an officer (in spite of my extensive college education), so I joined as an enlisted man. I was older and more educated than most of the people I met, except for the upper-level officers, and I didn't fit in very well. The officers wanted to befriend me, but protocol dictated that they shouldn't, because I was way down at the bottom of the pecking order. Many of the sergeants had difficulty telling me what to do because I was almost old enough to be their father. And me? Well, I had been a civilian too long. No matter how hard I tried, I just couldn't act like a naive eighteen-year-old again. "Fletcher," a friend jokingly said to me one day, "you don't have a military bone in your body."

I also had serious problems with the hierarchical arrangements of authority, the level of military spending and wastefulness, and the politics of defense policy. I worried more than once about being sent away from my family for several months to some distant place, all the while helping to prop up a government that never should have been in power in the first place. During my tour of duty, I began to realize that the only long-term way to achieve happiness with career and family was to have the freedom offered by self-employment.

It was when I was in journalism training at Fort Benjamin Harrison, Indiana, that Jan and I got the idea for our home business. There, I learned the techniques for putting newsletters together. I was amazed at just how simple it really was. One day, I came home from a class in layout and design and said, "Jan, do you realize how easy it would be for us to start a business putting newsletters together for other people?"

So there it was. The elemental part of our business had been born—and not a moment too soon, because hot on its heels came the birth of our second child. We decided to get going right away. I still had two years left to serve in the army, and we reasoned that if we started our business right away, it would be strong enough for me to join in full-time when I got out.

Once our business began to grow, we realized how impossible it would be to rein it in. What was supposed to have been a little part-time operation gradually took over our house and our lives. The struggle then became how to cope with all this new complexity we had created.

In the army, everything moved at a snail's pace. Although there were some very interesting things to do in my unit, there was, simply,

no war to fight. So, like firemen with no fires, we either practiced our skills or raked up pine needles. It was an abysmally slow existence. But when I arrived home in the evening, everything turned topsy-turvy. I went from a slow, uneventful, almost restful job to a chaotic home. Jan was so busy with the business that even if it had been her only job, it would have been nearly impossible for her to keep up with the work.

When I was stationed at Fort Bragg, North Carolina, we rented a little house with a tremendous yard. It's amazing to remember all the work that was done in that house. The neighbors must have thought we were crazy, the way we were always carrying boxes of stuff in and out. My fondest memories of the place are of coming home in the afternoon and walking back to the bedroom that we used as our office. Usually Jan would be back there working away, and the kids, all dressed up in crazy homemade costumes, would be busy making spaceships with their Legos. Jan and the kids would be off in the far end of the room, and between them and the door would be a veritable carpet of toys and cut-up pieces of paper. I got a lot of satisfaction from seeing those three significant others in my life stretching the limits of their knowledge and putting things together in new patterns. I loved the tremendous creative energy that went on in that office every day.

But there was a negative side to all of this change. Sometimes, after
the business got going, I felt resentful about my place in the home.
Although I had originally been 100 percent in favor of the idea and
was, in fact, the one who came up with the basic idea for our desktop
publishing system as well as the one who set it up, Jan was the one
who was getting all the credit. It was painful to hear her on the phone
saying, ". . .when I set up *my* business." I felt relegated to the position
of diaper changer and dish washer, while Jan was making a name for
herself on a national scale.

I was on a merry-go-round and I'd dropped the brass ring. Even
though I knew I should feel happy that Jan had managed to hang on
to *her* brass ring, I wanted a ring of my own. I just had to keep telling
myself, "Your time will come."

Although the business was growing when I left the army in late
1988, Jan was pregnant again. I was afraid we would not be able to
support ourselves solely with our business. We figured another year of
outside employment for me would be necessary. I felt like I was on
hold—not able to do the kind of work I really wanted to and yet not
able to commit wholeheartedly to an outside job, either. I was still not
able to get jobs that would pay a decent wage. Although I had a lot of
qualifications, I found that employers didn't want to hire me because
they didn't see me as a company man. I was too much the family man,
and I had a business of my own. When I interviewed for jobs of
importance, the question would inevitably come up: "How do you
feel about overtime?" I would always cut my own throat by saying:
"Overtime is OK from time to time, but my family is very important
to me, and I don't think routine overtime should be the norm." Then
everyone would be very polite and impressed with my résumé (after
all, you never can tell what the other applicants are going to be like),
but the job would go to someone else.

During this time, I did a lot of soul-searching. Why did I want to
work for myself, anyway? Was it the romantic memories of Jan and me
managing the inn? Or was it just my last resort before I gave up and
went for a job at the post office?

When I finally did get a job, at one of the largest software companies
in the world, I didn't get paid enough to support my family. In fact, if
it hadn't been for Jan's income from the business, we never would
have made it. I liked the work I was doing as a product support tech-

nician, but it was obvious that I would never get ahead financially until I joined my own business. It all boiled down to one basic fact: I had more freedom as a business owner than I did as an employee. A corporation pays the same to its employees no matter what the employees' situations are, but as a business owner, I could change our operation or even move to another location to make our business more profitable. I liked that. I'd rather work for myself and be responsible for the course of my life—good or bad—than have to cope with someone else's policies on parental leave, overtime, or whatever. And I certainly couldn't find better people to work with than my wife and three kids.

Before I joined the business, the biggest problem at home was that I rarely saw my kids between 7:00 a.m. and 6:00 p.m. I used to call the time between my arrival home and when the kids went to bed "the cranking hour," because frequently at that time those cute children would take off their cute suits and replace them with their evening grouch get-ups. Of course, this wasn't a daily occurrence (or I guess I would have gone totally crazy), but every time it happened, I'd look at Jan's back as she was slaving away trying to get a newsletter finished and feel frustrated that she was working so hard, yet the business was still too small for me to quit my job and help out.

Fathering in this situation was not easy. Even before we started our business, I found it difficult to stay in touch with my family while spending so many hours working away from home. But before we started the business, there was at least time in the evenings and on weekends to reconnect; also, during the day while I was at work, Jan could take the kids on trips to the beach or the playground.

However, after we started the business that family time was drastically reduced. Jan was occupied more and more with work; as a result, there were fewer trips to the playground. The kids didn't really understand the changes and responded to the situation by getting very rude and impatient at times. Before long, my time at home was transformed from an opportunity to reconnect with my family into a time to bring order out of chaos. I began to feel less like the loving father I wanted to be and more like a drill sergeant.

As a result, the kids started to feel like Dad was a real hassle to have around. I can remember one time when my son followed me around with a *Ghostbusters* ghost trap; every time I sat down, he would put it under my chair and try to suck me into the netherworld.

But that was the easy stuff. Sometimes the kids would behave really badly, seemingly destroying things out of resentment. I began to realize that the busier the home business got, the less time there was for reconnecting with the children as long as I still held a job outside the home. And the less time Jan and I spent reconnecting with our children, the harder they got to live with and the more firmly I was cast in the distasteful role of disciplinarian.

Now that I'm working at home, our kids are happier, they smile more when they see me, and for the most part the cranking hour has disappeared (although they still hate to go to bed). With Jan and I working together, business tasks are divided more equally, and the kids get more attention. My role as father is now less that of disciplinarian and more that of teacher.

When I was growing up, I never saw anybody work. I had no idea where my mother and father went after they left me at the baby-sitter's. I remember standing outside on the front porch when I was about four, looking off into the direction my father had gone and wondering if he was just on the other side of the hill, playing cards. I had no idea what work was, and it took many years of living as an adult before I really understood the concept. My kids will have no such questions. They've seen what I do and even participated in it within the scope of their abilities.

As a father working at home, I feel I have a much greater opportunity to teach and love my children than I could have had otherwise. It's been a tough row to hoe these past six years for everyone in the family, but I think we are stronger for the struggles we've endured together. What's more, we have built a life that is truly right for us.

17

LIFE ON THE DADDY TRACK

Randall Schultz

It's 6:45 on a chilly Albuquerque winter morning, and my heated
waterbed feels very cozy. My wife is already in the shower, and
despite the fact that my clock radio is doing its best to coax me awake,
I'd rather stay asleep for just a little longer. Then, from down the hall,
I hear a voice.

"Mommydaddy. Mommydaddy, I'm awake!"

With great difficulty, I pull myself out of bed and walk down the
hall. My two-year-old son is lying in bed, wrapped snugly in his favorite blanket. When he sees me, his face breaks into a smile.

"Daddy!" he says excitedly, holding out his arms to me.

I melt, just as I do every morning. As I pick him up and hold his
warm body in my arms, I thank God for the joy he has brought to my
family. I also congratulate myself on a decision I made which changed
my entire life.

It has now been more than a year since I left Southern California—
more than a year since I was last trapped in four-lane rush hour
traffic, since my toes danced in the chilly Pacific ocean, or since my
last smog alert. More importantly, it's been more than a year since I
quit a high-paying job as public relations director for a large real estate
management company and moved 1,000 miles and several life-styles
away. Even before the term "mommy track" was coined to describe
working women who have children, I had forsaken the world of corporate upward mobility in favor of the "daddy track."

But what motivates a rising young professional to leave a great job?
Why would a person want to move to a strange city and start a new
business from scratch? What makes a person change his entire world,
even when many of those who love him most tell him in serious tones
that he has lost his mind?

I can answer those questions with one word: Evan.

Evan was born when I was thirty-three years old, and he changed my life forever. I cut the umbilical cord that joined him to my wife. I was in the nursery and watched his first bath. I cried with him when he got his first shot. He was tiny, fragile, and wonderful, and he gave me new eyes with which to see the world. I soon realized that some of the things I had thought to be important in my life were keeping me very busy, but not making me particularly happy. When I looked into my son's eyes I could see, for the first time, that my life didn't have to revolve around my job. Evan's presence gave me a new set of priorities.

One day, when Evan was about four months old, I rose before the sun came up, showered, and got in my car for the long commute to work. As commutes go, this wasn't bad: a beautiful drive down the Pacific Coast Highway, nestled between the rolling hills and the rolling waves. But an accident had backed traffic up in Malibu, and my one-hour drive turned into an hour and a half. That afternoon there was a "crisis" at work which demanded my immediate attention. Now I don't even remember what it was, but at the time it seemed like an event of monumental proportions. I left work late, and didn't get home until well after dark.

I walked upstairs to Evan's room and crept in to watch him sleep. His tiny face was turned toward me, and I could see his lips move in a sucking motion. As I stood there in the dark, I realized my son hadn't seen me that day. I was gone when he awoke in the morning and was still gone when he went to bed. I had been working all day to provide for him but hadn't been a part of his life. The folly of my hard-working, long-distance commuting schedule suddenly became painfully obvious. Something had to change.

Despite my frenetic working schedule, and without my conscious awareness, in my heart I had already become one of America's growing number of "new" fathers. I grew up in the baby boom era, when fathers seemed to be away from home working all the time, except perhaps at the dinner hour. But new dads like myself wanted to be more than phantom fathers. We started getting involved in our kids' lives even before they were born. We attended Lamaze classes, and coached our spouses during childbirth. We read the books on child rearing and weren't afraid to change dirty diapers.

In truth, I was a daddy track father still trapped in a "Leave it to

Beaver" world. So when the folly of my long-distance commuting schedule became obvious and unbearable, I decided to make the biggest change in my life.

My wife, Virginia, and I had been looking for a new place to live for several years. We had watched the southern California that we knew when we were growing up, the southern California of orange groves and clear skies, gradually be replaced by one that was twice as big, with four times as many automobiles. During the period when I owned a nice foreign car, my stereo was stolen three times. On days when it was especially thick, the smog made me physically ill.

But Los Angeles is addictive. It's the last pit stop for the American Dream. The economy thrives, there is seemingly unlimited money to be made, and celebrities dine in every trendy Westside restaurant. Owning a home in the Los Angeles megalopolis is your ticket to the good life, and calculating how much your house is worth this month is the favorite pastime in the giant Monopoly game that constitutes life between Malibu and Manhattan Beach.

In spite of all this, the phrase "quality of life" gradually began to haunt me, because there seemed to be so little quality in my life. Then, suddenly, there was a baby in the family and not enough room in the house. Although our townhouse had appreciated dramatically, so had the larger houses we aspired to—right out of our reach. So we sold our home, pocketed our winnings, and bought a house in suburban Albuquerque, New Mexico.

Why Albuquerque? One reason was that it felt like a good, solid family town. The sky was blue, the air was clean, and the neighborhood was full of kids playing safely in the streets. Ironically, my new house is in a "Leave it to Beaver" kind of neighborhood, where people still borrow cups of flour from each other. But in my new life, nobody mistakes me for Ward Cleaver.

Now, instead of driving at least an hour to work and another hour or more back home, my office is a ten-second commute down the hallway. I've turned the back bedroom into a very workable office, complete with phone and computer. A fax machine and a photocopier will be added soon. The information revolution is here, and I'm in the middle of it.

I admit, my line of work lends itself well to flexibility. I can write advertising copy, press releases, magazine articles, and books just as well in my home office as I could in a big-city office building.

JILL FINEBERG

Assembly line auto workers don't have the same options. However, corporate America is beginning to offer more and more employees the choice to do some or all of their work at home. Home-based businesses are proliferating, particularly in large cities—so much so that entrepreneur Beth Smith publishes a bimonthly newsletter, *Business Line*, especially for people who operate businesses out of their homes. Today's dads and moms have new options to make a balanced work and family life a reality, and there will be even more flexibility in the future.

Interestingly, a tremendous desire is growing among parents—even those who might have been called "yuppies" a few years ago—to spend more time with their families. In a mid-1989 survey conducted by the major employment recruiter Robert Half, International, nearly eight out of ten Americans said they would sacrifice rapid career advancement in order to spend more time with their families. More than 74 percent of the men surveyed responded this way, and more than 54 percent of them said they would be willing to cut their work hours and salary up to 20 percent in order to have more family or personal time. Just a decade ago, such a consensus among males would have been unthinkable.

Such statistics make me feel considerably better about my personal decision to step off the fast track. At least now I know that I'm not some kind of freak. There are plenty of dads who want to do what I've done. They just haven't had the *chutzpa* to do it yet.

But there is an undeniable cost involved in all this. I did not make as much money in my first year as the sole proprietor of a communications business as I did in my last year as a corporate employee. I still won't make that much this year. But for a growing number of dads like myself, money is no longer the sole yardstick by which success is measured.

It doesn't show up as income in the checking account, but working in a home-based business gives me the reward of seeing Evan every day, through good times and bad, in sickness and in health. It's an adventure; each new day is different. I enjoy working for myself, and I enjoy breaking for lunch with Evan and Virginia, then walking back to my office to slave over my hot computer until dinnertime.

All right, I admit that this new situation isn't perfect. There are times when I wish I did have a distant office to escape to. Once in a while Evan gets to the phone before I do, and I then have to explain to a business client that he really isn't my secretary. Some of these clients probably think it's weird for me to be working in my home. But what do I care, as long as they respond to my invoices with checks?

Aside from a few minor inconveniences, life on the daddy track is everything I hoped it would be, and more. Evan just turned two, and I'm sure he doesn't understand how unusual it is to have Daddy at home during so much of the day, but he certainly has learned to take advantage of it. Until recently, I could retreat into my office, close the door, and be assured of a quiet place to work. Not anymore. A few months ago, he learned how to open the door, and he occasionally popped in to see how I was doing and to spread my paper clips all over the floor.

So I started locking the door. Now when he's bored with Big Bird or Bert and Ernie, he pounds on my door and yells, "Daddy, Daddy,

Daddy!!!!" Of all the words in the English language, Daddy may just be my favorite, so I almost always open the door. I give him a big hug, tell him that Daddy is working now, and send him on his way. Having done my fatherly duty, I can now return to my computer for nearly one minute of uninterrupted work.

Those of you who do not deal with a two-year-old on a daily basis may not realize that the average toddler has an I.Q. of approximately 175. This is a scientific fact, one which I am still trying to verify. My diminutive Einstein has devised all sorts of ploys to get me to open my office door.

Last week it was, "Daddy, Daddy, Daddy, dinner ready." He had me completely fooled. I picked him up and we trotted salivating into the kitchen. When I found out it was a false alarm, we had to console ourselves with Evan's favorite pre-dinner crackers.

Yesterday he pounded on the door crying, "Daddy, Daddy, ahboon popped!" I don't know what it's like at your house, but when an ahboon (translation: balloon) pops here, it's a 7.5 on the Richter scale. We hear about it for *months*. I dashed out of the office to console my shattered child, just as he dashed in to raid my paper clips.

But today's ploy was even more clever. "Daddy, Daddy, Daddy, I vacuum." I listened through the door for a moment, and sure enough, my wife was running the vacuum. I opened the door and Evan walked in, pushing his toy vacuum cleaner. It was so darn cute I let him throw paper clips all over the house.

Wait a second, someone's pounding on my door.

"Federal Express for Mr. Daddy."

Nah, it couldn't be.

PART IV:
FATHERING ALONE

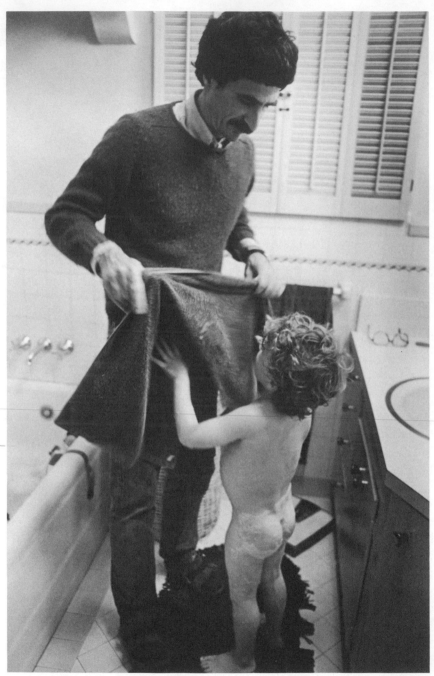

18

Noncustodial Fathers

Jack Maslow

Several years ago, my son and I were lying on his bedroom floor playing with his toys when he looked up at me and asked with all the innocence of a seven-year-old, "Daddy, what's total custody?" Needless to say, I was startled by the question and weakly responded with, "What do you mean?" "My mom says that she has total custody over me," he answered, "and that if you want to take me places, you have to ask for her permission." As the knot in my stomach grew tighter, I stumbled through a feeble explanation.

This was not the first time I had experienced the painful feelings of being the "out-parent," the feelings of somehow not being fully a part of my son's life. But believe it or not, this was the first time since the divorce five years earlier that the word "custody" had been mentioned. His mother and I never used the term. Custody was never an issue. We had a "good" arrangement in a pre-joint-custody era, one I had accepted because it seemed like the best option available, and one that allowed me a considerable amount of time with my son. Ours was a situation that impressed friends. Our arrangement looked and sounded better than those a lot of fathers had; my ex-wife and I were basically cooperative. I kept reminding myself of this, even when I was feeling greatly unappreciated and only halfway included in decision making. I needed to see my situation as special. The last thing I wanted to be was just another weekend father. Instead, I would be the ideal divorced father and would leave no room for criticism.

That conversation with my son helped me recognize that, regardless of what the arrangements were, being a noncustodial father was a painful experience for me, one fraught with feelings of uncertainty, exclusion, guilt, anger, and depression. Those feelings had always been there, but I had rarely admitted them, even to myself. If the pain did surface, I would express it in indirect ways and wait for it to bury itself again. I was not sure that I had the right to complain, or that anyone would want to hear my concerns.

My son was only two when his mother and I divorced. I missed being with him on a daily basis, but although I fantasized about being a full-time father, deep down I knew that I was not about to make any more changes that would further alter my world. I was grateful that his mother was there to see him through most of the day-to-day routines, so that I could be "out there doing what I was supposed to do." Nevertheless, I felt that I had to be "doing" more, and pressured myself to fit an image. As involved as I had been with my son in the intact family, I somehow felt I had to up that a notch post-divorce in order to prove to myself, my former wife, my son, and everyone else that I was still a real father.

I developed a living situation that assured proximity to my son and an ongoing active involvement in his life. While this was on the whole positive and important for our relationship, in retrospect it was also self-protective. By focusing my attention and energy on how I was supposed to be as a father, I could rationalize avoiding areas of personal change and growth. This perpetuated a sameness and predictability in my life which seemed necessary, but which also felt personally limiting. Still, I said to myself that no one would be able to say that I wasn't the perfect father, and that's what was really important.

As time went on, I became increasingly aware of my resentment at having to ask permission to do certain things with my son and at being governed by a legal document agreed to when I was most vulnerable. It made no sense to me. "Parents don't have to ask permission! Parents are parents. Period!"

I am quite fortunate that my son and I have developed a close, loving relationship, one that has blossomed into a secure friendship as he has reached his teens. For years, I feared that closeness could be easily lost. Because of my own insecurities and uncertainties, I walked on eggshells, not wanting to upset him and not sure that I even had the right to say "No". Gradually, I found that meeting new expectations does not always require sacrifice, but can actually be a way to achieve a rewarding sense of completeness and a new family feeling.

As noncustodial parents, we react to our situations with a wide range of behaviors and emotions. The desire for active involvement with our children may be present, but may be countered by self-doubt—often expressed in a father's tentativeness—and the uncertainties inherent in maintaining a "weekend" or "visiting father" attitude.

Often behavior can approach extremes, as when fathers emotionally or physically remove themselves. This, perhaps, reflects an attitude of: "I have given enough, now is the time for me." Some fathers allow the hurt and anger of divorce to linger and grow in ways that prove destructive to their relationships with their children. Other fathers feel so guilty and insecure that they develop an overdependence on their relationships with their children and place excessive burdens and expectations on them. This may be expressed as a need to be nurtured by one's children, or as a self-sacrificing feeling of "not having the right to do things for myself when I am not there to fully give to my children." Many fathers seek out the most expedient resolution: They become fixed or absolute in a situation that, ironically, requires ongoing flexibility and adaptability.

At stake here is the attainment of a sense of satisfaction, ideally achieved by balancing priorities so that the needs of both parent and child can be met. Children of divorce need and are entitled to continued positive involvement on the part of their fathers. Our culture has given us mixed messages on the priority of children in their fathers' lives, and perhaps as a result, we have tended to have minimal expectations in this area. The fact is that until recently, rewards for men have come strictly for academic and career pursuits, and not for providing emotional support and nurturance. Noncustodial fathers tend to see themselves as being in an inferior position and taken for granted. They are often perceived by others as wanting to do little more than meet their legal obligations as fathers.

Of course, why should someone receive recognition for something he is supposed to do? After all, single mothers are expected to provide care on a daily basis: they, too, develop feelings of self-sacrifice and resentment and must find ways of meeting parenting demands while still trying to conduct their own lives. Still, even when they recognize that this is so, those noncustodial fathers who do desire an active role as a post-divorce parent may continue to feel frustrated.

When their families break up, fathers are hit with an intense bombardment of feelings. Some may think that life will never get better. They may feel: "Why am I living alone? I really miss my kids! It doesn't make any sense!" The situation is confusing and gives rise to all sorts

JANET HOELZEL

of emotions. We are now single people, yet we are not really single.
Our friends without children are single people. Their responsibilities
are to themselves. We are family people, and yet not family people.
Friends who are still married are family people. So where do we fit in?
Many divorced fathers equate the move away from the family home as
an emotional as well as physical abandonment of their children—as a
betrayal of a commitment. At the same time, they may experience a
sense of freedom, of being out from under a heavy load. We feel bad
about leaving and guilty for feeling good about it. We are not sure
what we want, and the ambivalence may only get worse before it gets
better.

Few of us enjoy living with such contradictory feelings. Most of us
believe that our emotions should be harmonious. A key to resolving
this dilemma is to recognize that feelings and attitudes are not static.
They change continually. Overcoming upsetting, contradictory feelings is a process that requires time, patience, and commitment.

As divorced fathers, we can learn to be both parents and
individuals. We can develop independent relationships with our children that are linked neither to the pain of a difficult past nor to some

preconceived notion of what divorced parenting is supposed to be.

To do this, we must be open to recognizing how our attitudes and behaviors affect our children and to discovering ways to deal with our feelings constructively. We *can* stop viewing ourselves as victims, or as being in an inferior position. Many fathers who feel uncertain, or who are so caught up in their own insecurities that they resentfully accept a passive role, benefit from the opportunity to talk and share feelings. This sharing can lead to new options for experiencing a more active parenting role. There is no reason for children to expect less from divorced fathers, or for fathers to play less of a role in their children's lives. We must explore ways of developing and maintaining relationships with our children that can grow and change with the years.

Being a divorced, noncustodial father may be a statement of fact, but it need not be a state of mind. Terms such as "weekend dad" reflect attitudes as much as reality. More and more divorced fathers are moving forward in a constructive manner and finding that they can make themselves more emotionally available to their children, while still pursuing other important relationships and goals in their lives.

What can we as divorced fathers do? What are the options and the possibilities? Here are some important considerations:

1) Remember that a divorce is between spouses, not between parent and child. Do not be afraid to tell your children you love them. Show them how you feel. Don't back away from them: be with them.

2) Aim to normalize your relationships with your children and to develop a new family system that is independent of what you had as an intact family. Once you can do this, both the work and the fun begin. This means making the children an active part of your life, creating a home atmosphere that is both warm and inviting, and taking an interest in what your children are doing in their daily lives. This will help to minimize the disruption for everyone, and to build something new for your children and yourself.

3) Realize that your children need you and that you need them. As a father, you have a great deal to contribute to their development, and there is much pleasure to be derived from knowing that your presence has made a difference. Their presence will also make a difference for you. Sharing in school projects, buying clothes, attending various activities, knowing their friends, getting caught up in family squabbles, preparing meals together, kissing the children goodnight and

tucking them into bed—all create the togetherness of a family unit. Divorce may be a painful process, but the more we commit ourselves to our continued parenting, the faster any pain can heal.

4) Listen to your children's concerns, even when what they say may hurt. Their feelings are legitimate and need to be expressed, since they, too, have just experienced a great upheaval. Allow for sharing of emotions and for differences of opinion. Our children know that we care and that we are actively present in their lives when we share with them.

Becoming a divorced parent is often a scary and disorienting experience. It challenges feelings of competence in otherwise very competent people. What we, as individuals, are working toward is reestablishing an inner balance, so that we may feel less victimized and develop a greater sense of our personal power. What we and our children are working toward is feeling comfortable with one another in a new situation and setting the groundwork for the years ahead. This may feel awkward or even awful at first, but it is important to remember that life will get better: although they will be different from what they were before, circumstances will eventually be better than they are now. Confusion and uncertainties will be replaced with feelings of assuredness and competence as we move to develop and enhance our skills as parents. The decision to remain connected and active with our children will pay off in a greater sense of fulfillment, a heightened sense of self-worth, a deep satisfaction in being a part of our children's lives, and in the intrinsic reward of knowing that we have done the best that we can as parents.

For More Information

Greif, G. L. *Single Fathers*. Lexington, MA: Lexington Books, 1985. This study of the experiences of 1,100 custodial fathers addresses many of the issues faced by single fathers.

Ricci, I. *Mom's House, Dad's House*. New York: Collier Books, 1980. An excellent book on shared parenting and joint custody after a divorce.

Shephard, M., and G. Goldman. *Divorced Dads: Their Kids, Ex-Wives and New Lives*. Radnor, PA: Chilton Books, 1979. This hard-to-find but good book, written for fathers by two divorced fathers, may have to be ordered directly from the publisher: Chilton Books, Chilton Way, Radnor, PA 19089; 215-964-4729.

Wallerstein, J., and J. Kelly. *Surviving the Breakup*. New York: Basic Books, 1980. Probably the most popular resource for both the professional and lay community, this work is considered a major reference in divorce research.

Ware, C. *Sharing Parenthood After Divorce*. New York: Bantam Books, 1984. A good look at shared parenting.

Hill, G A. *Divorced Father*. White Hall, Va.: Betterway Publications, Inc. 1989. A good and practical book on being a divorced father. Deals with a variety of ongoing issues faced by fathers and their children.

19

CHILD SUPPORT THAT REALLY IS

Bruce Low

Some relationships do not survive, even though both partners had the best intentions. We are all familiar with the depressing statistics on divorce, single-parent households, and the numbers of children affected when their parents part company. There is no need to repeat the "bad news"; instead, let's make the situation as good as possible for the children who survive the wreckage.

My story started out no different from many others. My ex-wife and I met, came to love each other, and found ourselves, four years later, with an eighteen-month-old son and unresolvable problems that were driving us apart. The question was no longer whether or not we could continue the marriage but rather how to salvage our good individual relationships with our child despite the divorce.

As a noncustodial father, I needed to consider two essential issues: visitation and child support. My overriding concerns in child support were a safe place for my son to live and play, and a secure home environment for his emotional support and growth. Since my son is very important to me, both as a person and as a legal responsibility, I chose to provide a combination of fairly generous child support and conservative, short-term, contractual alimony. This arrangement allows me to meet several important goals beyond those which the courts actually require.

Because my son's physical safety is a prerequisite for all other considerations, the alimony I pay is in the form of continued payments on the newest car my wife and I had, the car with the greater crash survivability and lower probability of breakdown. The alimony will last until the automobile is paid for, and the car should be reliable well beyond that point.

I was also convinced that my son needed his mother full-time to ensure his proper emotional growth as a secure, well-adjusted, mature man. He had been the focus of our life as a couple after he was born, and we agreed that this would continue to be the case for each of us separately but that his mother would be the full-time nurturer. It was a pragmatic decision. First of all, he was still breast-feeding; second, it would be easier for me to maintain an income large enough to share than for her to establish one. As a midlevel technical manager, I would be able to support both them and myself on my salary. Inflation will erode her child support to the point that my ex-wife will probably have to return to work once my son starts school. However, the financial underpinning I provide will allow her to choose work with flexible hours.

The amount of child support provided was based on actual requirements. What was needed was a neighborhood secure from random violence, where the yards would be fenced for safe play and where good schools would be available once my son grew old enough to attend them. A neighborhood with features such as this commands a hefty rent in my city. In addition, other expenditures, such as those for food, insurance, and clothing, were needed for my ex-wife and son to live safely and reasonably comfortably. The total, about $1,650 a month, now comes "off the top" of my pay after all deductions. This amounts to 65 percent of my take-home pay every month, or approximately seven times as much as the average local court-ordered amount.

Living off the remainder is not very comfortable and brings constant money worries. There are no hidden assets, no outside income, and no special tax benefits to paying child support as opposed to alimony. Nor was I prepared for the confusing reaction of new women in my life to my decision. They think that what I am doing is "beautiful," but still expect to be courted and entertained as if money were no object! Reaching a level in a new relationship where marriage is a possibility can easily cause these issues to come to a head. They have already become a major stumbling block. It will take a very nontraditional woman to accept this situation without resentment, a woman who will agree to being the major breadwinner in the relationship. I have not yet met one.

Substantial child support does not legally "buy" anything when it comes to the issue of visitation. In every jurisdiction that I have studied, the issues of child support and visitation are always con-

sidered separately. But although large child support cannot "win" anything, it also cannot hurt. After all, many visitation problems arise
from hard feelings related to too little child support, or from nonpay-
ment controversies. Removing this sore point allows the remainder of
a relationship to flow more smoothly.

In my case, the divorce decree allows for only fifteen hours of visitation per week, spread over a minimum of three periods. This has, in
actuality, expanded to include daily visits Monday through Thursday
and full weekends. There is, generally, a positive relationship between
me and my ex-wife; we recognize that our son needs both a mother
and a father. And, of course, I demonstrate my good intentions every
payday!

It makes no difference to me whether or not my ex-wife is grateful
for the amount of child support I give her. I am only supporting her
indirectly; I am really supporting my son. It is right for me to live like
this for now. As a result, my influence on my son extends beyond my
daily visits into what I do to support his entire environment, even
when he is not with me. Put as simply as possible, I continue to love
my son very much. I am trading my current comfort for his future.
Parents have done this throughout history. None of us has ever
wanted a medal; we do it because we love our kids.

My experience has meaning for every papa in a troubled marriage.

Do not let your anger and frustration hurt your children if you divorce. If your children already live apart from you, you can increase your support any time you wish by paying more than the court has required. You may even offer to let your ex-wife have the divorce decree rewritten to legally increase the amount.

Maintain contact with the children of your body and soul. Support them as much as you can in every area. They will benefit, and you will grow as a man.

20

SINGLE FATHER, SINGLE PARENT, PARENT

William F. Van Wert

There was nothing natural-feeling about my becoming a single parent. Instead, I felt at first as though I had been tossed around in a whirlpool. The birth of my third son preceded the death of my mother from cancer by two weeks. From the start, the new baby was up every night, crying from the pain of ear infections. After nine months of "pink medicine" (Amoxicillin), our doctor determined that he should have tubes put in both ears. At that point, my ex-wife went into an emotional and physical tailspin and was advised by her therapist to leave her family for her mental health. This same therapist told me bluntly, regarding my children, "It's you or foster homes."

So there I was, still grieving over a dead mother and now grieving over a departed wife. Suddenly, I was, as well, the single father of three boys under five: two still in diapers, two still bottle-feeding. I had no immediate family in the area where we lived; no support group; no baby-sitters; and, obviously, no role models.

I did have a few things going for me. First, I was a tenured full professor, well established in my career. My two-day teaching schedule allowed me to minimize on day care, baby-sitters, and time away from the boys. Second, my wife and I had had our children at home, so I was already incredibly bonded with my boys. Third, the grief over my mother's death was accompanied by a clarity of vision (albeit temporary) about what really mattered and what didn't in daily life. In retrospect, I can be grateful for these things. At the time, I had no idea how much they counted.

I would like to say I took on the role of single father gracefully, but I didn't. At the time, I had an image of parenting which told me that children needed their mothers, not their fathers. I had little self-esteem, felt rejected, and was so out of touch with my psyche that

I didn't even know how I felt from one moment to the next. I sighed a lot, made lists and lost them, talked to myself, cried some. I was a horror in the kitchen. My eldest son, Ian, who was four at the time, knew the difference between food that was burned and food that was not. While he wouldn't condemn my cooking, he wouldn't lie about it either. "You tried," he would say, while urging his younger brothers, David and Daniel, to give my spaghetti attempts a second chance.

My father came to visit me during this time. He was supposed to stay a week; he stayed two days. I found him with tears in his eyes and asked him what was the matter. "This is not man's work," he said. I resented that. My therapist told me my kids would probably be "damaged" kids. I resented that, too. I resented the ineptitude of men in general and my own ineptitude; their aloofness, my aloofness; their foolish pride, my foolish pride. Other men avoided me: at least, they avoided my single-parenthood. I think they found me threatening. This made me laugh, because I felt anything but. Women found me "noble", or at least, what I was doing to be noble; another laugh, because I wasn't feeling noble at all. I think my presence often made them resent their own husbands, because I was both holding a job and raising children. One mother told me: "Women are always single-parenting, even in their marriages, but a man . . ." These women judged my ex-wife even more harshly than I did.

Some things actually became easier. There were no more arguments about whose turn it was to cook, do laundry, grocery-shop, or walk the crying baby. It was always my turn. No more awkwardness about whether to spend the late evenings relating to another adult or prepare my classes. The time after my children went to sleep was suddenly all my time. After orchestrating order for my sons all day, at night I would sit alone at my typewriter, no inspiration left for any great writing, and just let feelings of chaos wash over me. I worried about money. I worried that I might never feel sexual again. I worried that my boys would grow up to be gay from too much father-exposure. Often I would break down and cry, then try to harden myself; neither posture worked very well. If I gave in to sadness, it weakened me physically. If I didn't give in, I felt numb emotionally. There were terrible bouts of a kind of loneliness I had never faced before. I realized that I had been in some sort of relationship with a girlfriend, lover, or wife from the eighth grade to the age of thirty-five, and I didn't really know what it meant to be fully alone. I scared myself. I bored myself. Stubbornly, I sat with myself night after night until my time alone didn't bother me any more. My reasoning was: If I couldn't learn to enjoy being with myself, how did I expect anyone else to enjoy being with me?

It was during those first two years of single fatherhood that I stopped feeling like a victim of my circumstances and started realizing that I really liked being a dad full-time. I looked forward to the middle-of-the-night ritual of walking the baby, singing him songs, and feeling him fall asleep at my neck, only then to have David wake up, needing a change, a bottle, walking, or singing. It was not unusual for me to wake in the morning and find all three of my sons asleep in my bed. I took strength from little things they said. One day, Ian told me: "Daddy, everything you say and do is right and true." The fact that it rhymed gave it the ring of prophecy.

We read books, and when I got bored with them, I would invent new dialogue. I did this until one of my kids finally said: "Daddy, Babar doesn't talk like that." We made up ditties, the grosser the better, for long car rides. At the risk of offending some readers, I offer the most famous of these:

> Who put those poops
> in my ice-cream scoops?
> Chocolate-y gloops.
> ~~I ate those two brown poops.~~
> Whoops.
> BLEAH!

We all screamed the BLEAH! as loud as we could, then laughed. Within minutes, one of the boys would suggest singing it again.

Each time we took a trip somewhere, I packed twenty to thirty bottles of milk and/or juice, which were usually finished off in the first two hours. I often found myself changing diapers on the turnpike turn-outs or on top of picnic tables at rest areas. I didn't care. I was determined that we should take these trips, and after each one, I gained new confidence for the next.

Some of our favorite memories of those outings are of motel stops around the Midwest. The first time Ian saw the hygienic display of paper across a toilet seat, he declared that these were "slingshots for doodies, so that lazy maids wouldn't have to clean the toilets." Sometimes we used the motel beds as trampolines. We had pillow fights

and stayed up late, running racehorse through all the cable channels
—all the things we didn't do at home.

When fathering became fun like that, I realized we were all healthy
enough for me to leave the boys from time to time for a lecture, a
movie, or even a date. What held me back was that I had not yet, after
almost three years of single-parenting, tapped into that rich resource
of information and support: the neighborhood mothers' network.
Here was a twenty-four hour hotline of crackerjack parents who knew

the available pool of baby-sitters backward and forward; who knew about day care, toys, secondhand clothing stores, museums to see, and all the free or cheap entertainment available on weekends. I knew who these women were; I just hadn't had the courage to approach them. Finally, I put my pride and embarrassment aside and called them. I needn't have waited so long. I found them surprised, sympathetic, and very helpful and began to team up with some of them on visits to the zoo, arboretum, and mall. From sharing such trips to sharing confidences—horror stories of divorce, financial woes, parenting styles, even gossip—was an easy slide.

I found these contacts to be refreshingly non-judgmental and uncharged sexually. At first, I worried a little about the latter aspect of my new relationships. Was I so beaten-down a parent-person that I had become somehow desexed without even knowing it? But then I realized that I was relating to women in a very new way: casually, without posturing, innuendo, or other assertions of sexual difference. I was making friends with women, lots of women all at once. Furthermore, I realized there were a great many single-parent families all around me, and I was no longer the exception, or leper, among them.

Still, I found dating again to be difficult, awkward, sometimes even silly. One women proposed to me on our first date because she liked the looks of my sons. Another asked me to make a baby with her. Others, who accurately tabbed me as a caretaker, were frustrated at my unwillingness to take care of them. They didn't understand that I had three children to meet my caretaking needs, much of my touching needs, and some of my conversation needs.

Some women were put off if I canceled a date when one of my boys got sick. Some of these women were, themselves, single parents. I thought they would have understood that children come first, adults second, but they didn't. One even offered her own willingness to go out despite having a sick child at home as a role model that I should emulate; if I didn't, it meant that I didn't care for her, not that I was being a good parent.

In fact, it was not uncommon for me to question why I was going out at all. The energy it took to arrange for the sitter, see to the boys' needs, get dressed up and "psyched up" for going out was sometimes too much, especially when I yawned on dates, missed the boys, or worried about the money I was spending. What was true at the time was that I was over-sensitive about being a single parent, and that I took the "parent" part more seriously than the "single" part. In fact, I never believed in the single part. If you're a parent of small children, whether you're separated or divorced or widowed, you're not truly single. You and your kids come as a package.

I have been single-parenting for ten years now. When I look back on the first five years, I do so with nostalgia, but also with horror and amazement. I loved my boys inordinately as babies, but I don't understand how I got through that time, or how life got to feel normal and good along the way. I suspect there's a certain amount of healthy unremembering or downright forgetting involved here, similar to the way people forget much of pregnancy and the pain of labor once the baby has come.

I always felt my priorities to be family first, then work, then self. There's not always much left over by the time one gets to the self. While I was married, I maintained a deliberate distance between my public life and private life. With single-parenting, much of what was private became public, and much of the public life was exposed as a posturing and a mask. I'm convinced that these same shifts in priorities happen in two-parent families as well: they just seem to be accelerated or exaggerated for single parents.

I don't put homilies up on the refrigerator or bulletin board, but I do keep them in my mind, especially when they can give me an extra incentive to accomplish or endure something. During those first five years of single-parenting, I constantly had some old saying playing in my head. When I couldn't rationally figure out the failure of my marriage, but also couldn't afford to let it depress me too much, I remembered a Willie Nelson line from the film *Barbarosa*: "What cannot be changed must be endured." A Japanese haiku also proved apt: "Even with devils, we prefer the ones we're used to." Ditto a cliché from my grandmother, uttered often when I was growing up: "Play the cards you're dealt." When I felt victimized and angry at my ex-wife for her freedom and lack of responsibility, I remembered a line from Maya Deren's book on Haitian voodoo, *The Divine Horsemen*: "Great gods won't mount little horses." Or the ditty my boys used to say when they decapitated dandelions: "Mommy had a baby and her head popped off." Or the old saying: "What goes around comes around." And when I felt drained to a stupor, I remembered again what Ian had told me when he was four: "Daddy, everything you say and do is right and true."

I still regret that there were no male role models for me, but in retrospect, I understand that I used my mother as a role model. She raised seven children, so who was I to squawk at raising three? Women can be wonderful role models for men if they can put their male pride aside. I also finally forgave my father his absenteeism, emotional distance, and inability to help me, and, having done that, I forgave myself those same things as well.

There is no shortage of places to put blame for this male patterning and need for late forgiveness. The culture is to blame. Religions are to blame. High schools could easily push boys to take home economics instead of shop or mechanical drawing. Even Hollywood is to blame. I thought the movie *Kramer vs. Kramer* was a fairy tale for fools, full of lies and over simplifications. And after my boys had seen *Three Men and a Baby*, I asked them when they thought Hollywood would be ready for *One Man and Three Babies?*

Different men have confided in me, "I would leave my marriage, but I wouldn't know how to cook or do for myself." And, "I would leave my marriage, but she would move and then I'd lose sight of the kids." And, "I would leave my marriage, but I wouldn't know how to handle the kids on my own." There is tragedy in these confessions. Most men are still willing to accept their own ineptitude, willing to believe in the primacy of the mother, and willing to keep the mother as a buffer between them and their children. Men can't biologically birth children, but they can psychologically own those births. Put more simply, children need parents, not genders. It's taken me ten years, but I have finally learned to dissolve "single father" into "single parent" and "single parent" into just "parent." To make the single father a symbolic or mythic figure is, finally, a false romanticism of the worst sort.

At this writing Ian is thirteen, David is eleven, and Daniel is nine. I'm two months shy of having three boys in double digits. I now find parenting easier mechanically—the boys know how to cook, do laundry, and grocery-shop—and harder psychologically. Ian now wants more privacy and less affection from me. David is in a collector phase; baseball cards are his current passion. Daniel tries to charm and manipulate me into letting him stay overnight at his friends', or buying him treats, or upping his allowance.

I find it harder to stay ahead of my sons. I realize, fait accompli, that they're watching too much TV, not eating enough vegetables, and stalling on their homework as a way to delay bedtime. I've had two "birds and bees" talks. I feel like their chauffeur, their authority figure to rebel against, and their foil. I reproach myself for not taking enough pictures, for hurrying bedtimes, and for not being able to afford better vacations. I don't take them to the library enough; I haven't insisted that they keep taking violin lessons; I forget sign-ups for Little League. I yell too much; I forget to get them bubble baths or to light candles to make supper more attractive. Our apartment seems to shrink as they grow and take up more space. In short, I've got a bunch of teenagers around me. If all this sounds like what any parent of teenagers would be going through, it's because it is.

I suspect a homophobia inherited from our culture makes many fathers feel constrained from touching their children. I'm happy to say I just don't have that hang-up. I lay on hands whenever I can—hug them when they let me, wrestle with them as a substitute for hugging, give them back massages or foot massages at bedtime when their guard is down. I listen to them and encourage everything from conversations about their day to singing, acting out, playing cards, and working at my typewriter or computer. I shift tactics and change rules when previous tactics and rules don't work. I apologize and ask their forgiveness when I screw up. I don't send them to their rooms; don't insist that they finish their plates; don't let them get me interested in who actually started a given fight; don't let them pit me against their mother, or one of them against the other. I encourage their independence, preach respect and friendship in their relationships, and try to keep their stress to a minimum and their sense of humor strong, collectively and individually. Instead of making them feel guilty for certain behavior, I make workable contracts with them: for example, for their promise not to do drugs they can wear their hair however they please and put whatever rock posters on their walls they wish. I don't censor what I don't like. Instead, for example, I try to get Ian to translate Easy E's rap music into English I can understand or get Daniel to sing a heavy metal song for me. I don't pretend that any of these things are what all parents should do; they're just some of the things I do that seem to work.

Parenting is one of those outside-inside, caterpillar-butterfly propositions. If you're on the outside looking in, it looks like drudgery, with lots of pain and disappointment and few tangible rewards. If you're actually doing it, it's very difficult to explain the joy of it to someone on the outside. At this point, I parent just to parent: one of those statements that sounds redundant but isn't. I choose it, am glad for it most of the time, and find it the most satisfying thing I've ever done.

I realize also that parenting is a privilege, a temporary privilege. I'm only beginning to realize *how* temporary now that my boys are becoming teenagers. My sons owe me nothing for the privilege I have had in parenting them. Nothing. I get what I get from doing it, with no deferred debts. I don't know how better to explain this than to use an analogy a librarian friend gave me: Children are like books on loan, books we can enjoy but never keep. We can lose the books, we can not read them during the time allotted, we can hold onto them after their due date and pay the penalty, but none of these ploys changes the basic fact that they're on loan. The consolation is this: We can keep the enjoyment, if not the books themselves.

PART V:
REMEMBERING OUR OWN FATHERS

21

CELEBRATE FATHER'S DAY

Samuel Osherson

"I haven't seen my father in over two years. Things have never been great between us," the Los Angeles TV studio technician confessed earnestly. "He's seventy years old, and next month the whole family is getting together in New York on Father's Day for a celebration." He pauses, then asks shyly: "Do you think I ought to fly back for it?"

"What do you want to do?" I inquire.

"I want to go, but do you think he wants me to?"

"I'll bet he wants you to, even if he can't say it."

Obviously encouraged, this burly, forty-year-old man shakes my hand with gratitude and wonders, "You mean it's worth the money for the airfare?"

Distance and mystery characterize many normal men's relationships with their fathers. Often, this aloofness hides the deep yearning they feel for a reconciliation with them.

The arrival of Father's Day each year provides an opportunity to reflect on the unfinished business between men and their fathers. Many men today are rediscovering their fathers, traditionally the "invisible" family members.

Father's Day in my childhood is a dim, vague memory. Mother's Day produced flowers, often breakfast in bed. Father's Day begat maybe a card, usually purchased by my mother and dutifully signed by us all. A forty-year-old lawyer looked puzzled when asked how his family celebrated Father's Day. Finally he said, "The men in my family were not supposed to need anything, so we didn't do very much at all for my father. For a long time, I assumed my father didn't want direct expressions of caring. Finally, I've begun to realize how important it is for both of us to find a way to express how much we matter to each other." For many sons, this process does not really start until they become adults. Fathers and sons are not usually accustomed to direct expressions of affection, and thus do not often develop a common language for talking together and sharing concerns.

A thirty-five-year-old son, the vice-president of a bank, haltingly talked of not seeing his father for over a decade, until the old man was near death. "He was dying of cancer and he came to *my* house for the final weeks of his life. I took care of him; I bathed him and fed him until the end." One painful fact held the banker in its grip: "Those weeks together went by, then he died, and I never heard him say, 'I love you.'" Remembering, he broke into tears.

In recent years, I have talked to and about many fathers and sons in the course of my work. I have found that a central task for men today is to come to terms with the heroism and failure in our fathers' lives and to decipher how our relationships with them have shaped our identities as men. The traditional physical or psychological absence of fathers from families creates a normal sense of loss and yearning in sons. The midlife years are often the time of a search for reunion between grown sons and aging fathers.

"Men don't talk about their feelings" is the common stereotype, but men will talk about their fathers if given a sympathetic hearing. They may talk shyly or brusquely, often in the tentative, wary tone some men use to give voice to their most profound feelings. They may be men who feel sorrowfully alienated from their fathers, men whose fathers have died, men whose fathers left the family years ago, or new fathers yearning for a sign of affirmation from their own families as they strive to be more available and flexible than their own fathers were.

In Philadelphia on a recent Father's Day, a local men's center constructed the world's largest Father's Day card at a nearby museum. Wall-sized canvas sheets were stretched so that fathers and children could impress their handprints on them and sign, "Happy Father's Day." The card was then presented to the city, and the event enshrined in the *Guinness Book of World Records*. The project captured the yearning many fathers feel for recognition of their presence in the family: it was a concrete manifestation of their often unspoken love for their families.

For many men, though, the struggle for connection is more silent and lonely. "I haven't seen my biological father in fourteen years, since our parents divorced," a twenty-nine-year-old son related sadly. "Should I call him? I have a son now, and I want him to know his grandfather." Grown men of divorced families often have painful thoughts about their biological fathers. By a year after the divorce, 50 percent of fathers have no contact with their families.

"What do you want to do?" I inquired.

"I want to see him," the man continued eagerly, "but what if he's not interested in me?" He hesitated, then revealed more of his conflict. "I have a stepfather, whom I love. Will he take it as a reflection on him if I call my father?"

Grown children of divorced families often carry a sense of responsibility, feeling that the breakup was somehow their fault and wondering whether or not their father really cares about them. When they have a stepfather, many sons will feel caught between their fathers, as if caring about one is a betrayal to the other. Yet, sons need to know *all* their fathers. The wish to find a lost father does not reveal lack of love for a stepfather: rather, it is a normal developmental step taken as a person matures. The love for both fathers may be increased by a son who finds and de-idealizes his biological father.

Often men will say, "I can't call my father, I don't know how to make contact." One son who had not seen his father in years called him out of the blue: "We sat there silently on the phone, not knowing what to say to each other." Sudden phone calls may leave both parties feeling on the spot. A letter is often an easier ice-breaker. The son or father may write openly that he is thinking of the other, wondering if he thinks of him, and feeling that he would like to see him, and hoping that the other feels the same way.

The death of a father is a milestone in a man's life. Freud described the death of his father as the most important and poignant loss of his life. Yet, when a father dies, things are not necessarily over between father and son. The task often remains of transforming the memory of a judgmental, critical, or disappointing father into a more caring, nurturing, and supportive image. The son can enlarge his vision of his father from the narrow, one-dimensional picture he saw as a child.

Sons can do this by coming to understand their fathers as real people, caught within the pressures and conflicts of the male role. Some sons have described finding and reading their fathers' journals and diaries, glad to have been able to learn directly about the feelings and lives of their fathers. Others have extended their understanding by

talking to their fathers' peers and relatives. Often, business associates tend to know a father better than his own son did. The search is to find and hold on to the thread of goodness and caring within the lost father.

A mathematician related to me that when he was a teenager, his father seemed to disappear emotionally from his life. This caused a deep wound for the growing boy. After his father's death, his mother gave the grown man his father's journal. "I read, to my shock, that when I was fifteen my father was fired from his job for union organizing. He was so shamed by this that he never told his children, and then he began to work three part-time jobs to support the family. He was working from 8:00 a.m. to 10:00 p.m. all those years. Seeing the burden of vulnerability, shame, and love for us that my father struggled with makes me feel much more connected to him. I can see how similar he and I actually are."

A son can visit his father's grave, bringing flowers or the words he always wanted to say, and imagine his father's loving response at the scene. Sons describe writing letters to their dead fathers, letters that will never be sent but nevertheless permit them to say what needs to be said and to imagine their fathers' response.

The very same struggles extend to men whose fathers are alive. In a sense, all men lose their fathers and must regain them as they age. A lawyer observed, "My father gets angry every year around Father's Day. He starts criticizing me; he won't open the presents I buy for him. He's unused to all the attention, and something in it feels dangerous to him." Often, when sufficient emotional space has not developed between men and their fathers, tender feelings cannot emerge. The lack of a common language can carry into their adult relationship.

Many families develop expressions of caring on Father's Day— treasured rituals and family events. However, for some children, these family events tend to have a surface quality. In the words of one fifty-year-old man, "It was as if we could never say how important Dad was or really talk about what was going on in the family."

The absence of a common language for affection and caring between fathers and sons implies that such a language needs to be developed in the adult years. One grown son was shocked to hear his father confess, "I never knew how to be both your father and your friend when you were young." Another son lamented, "I know how to drive my father away, but not how to draw him close."

A great deal depends on how sons approach their fathers. One executive described how his strategies changed: "My father was pretty distant. One holiday, after months of obsessing about it, I went home and said, 'Dad, there are these things I want to talk about—we've never been close, you're always at work, and I'm worried you're going to die and we'll have worked nothing out.' He looked at me with his eyes wide open and said, 'You're crazy. I don't want to talk about all that, forget it,' and he walked out of the room."

Later adulthood is a hard time to unlearn psychological defenses, particularly when sons approach their fathers with a heavy agenda, as if their fathers were armored forts to be stormed by determination. The executive continued, "What worked better for me was when I said, 'I just want you to know I love you.' Later that evening he came over to me when I was reading the newspaper. He leaned over and hugged me and said, 'I love you, too.' "

Men often underestimate how far fathers will go for them. Fathers, as they age, need a sense of reconciliation as much as sons do. In later adulthood a father wants to know that his life makes sense, that the wounds of the past are healed, and that, as one father told his grown child, "We can all forgive and forget. It's all OK between us."

Achieving a sense of reconciliation does not require an airing out of all the psychological dirty laundry in a family, nor does it imply a father and son becoming buddy-buddy in a superficial friendship. It simply means that a father and son come to see that the wounds of the past are healed and that there is some common ground and shared struggle between them, as well as mutual respect and appreciation.

Building bridges involves overcoming your fears of each other. It is surprising how often sons will block their fathers' attempts at reconciliation. Fathers and sons are often scared of their anger at each other and of the common sadness that they share. A successful forty-year-old trial lawyer mentioned that on weekends when he visited his parents, he drove repeatedly past their house if his mother's car was not in the driveway, because he was afraid to be alone with his father.

Many fathers are also afraid of their sons. Sons represent mortality. They are symbols of the future to men who are struggling with aging and their own sense of obsolescence.

Sons who have taken the emotional role of surrogate husband to their mothers often carry a good deal of shame and fear. As one man recalled, "After all, I did prefer my mother." When the time comes to resurrect our fathers, we may fear their final accusation of our betrayal of them.

A son may also need to acknowledge his secret wish to place responsibility for his life at his father's feet. Many sons hold onto the fantasy that if only their fathers would change, then their own life would be better.

Some sons, because they have so much to say themselves, talk at their fathers rather than hear how much their fathers themselves are actually saying. Instead, a son might ask his father about his work and what he loved about it; about his family, his disappointments and satisfactions and what he would do differently; and about what he feels most proud of having accomplished in his life. Sons need to ask questions about their fathers' lives and truly listen to the answers. This way, we may see that our fathers were also sons who struggled with *their* fathers.

We can expand our understanding of our fathers by listening to them. What is most important is enhancing our inner image of our fathers so that it may become fuller and richer, thereby freeing ourselves of the one-dimensional picture we were afforded in childhood. Mark Twain summarized this well: When he left for college at age seventeen, his father seemed to be a dunce. When he returned home at twenty-one, he could hardly believe how much his father had learned.

Remember that if you fail once at establishing communication, you have not necessarily failed forever. Fathers and sons mellow as they age, and new opportunities arise. The key is to leave the door open. Evelyn Waugh was very insightful when he wrote, "The proper relationship between father and son as they age is as guest and host."

22

LESSONS MY FATHER TAUGHT ME

Stephen Barlas

On weekday afternoons in 1967, when everyone else's father was locked inside the "nine-to-five" prison, my dad made regular jailbreaks to the rutted asphalt tennis courts at Long Island's Carle Place High School.

I could not relax until he arrived. My nerves were more tightly strung than the gut in my wooden Wilson Kramer tennis racket, and I repeatedly looked over my shoulder, straining to see if the family Pontiac Catalina, with its black-wall tires, had lumbered into the school parking lot.

Spectators rarely came to our tennis matches. At Carle Place High, like every other school, football was king. Excited parents—even the mothers and fathers of my tennis teammates—jammed the football stadium stands on Saturdays. In those years before Connors and McEnroe, high school tennis drew sneers, not cheers.

Tennis' stigma never stopped Dad from attending all my matches, both home and away. Though the hour and the day were always inconvenient, he broke away from his civil engineering business in Queens. He never said why he came so religiously to watch me play, and I never asked for a reason.

On his way from the parking lot, he dodged skirted field-hockey players on their way to practice. It was hard to tell which was shorter, his crew cut or their freshly mowed playing field. Other fathers were letting their hair grow long, but being "mod" was not important to Dad, nor was having white-wall tires. *Being there*—lugging a crumpled grocery bag filled with Hershey bars for our team—was.

When my father finally reached the 25-foot-high mesh fence that enclosed the four tennis courts, he crammed three fingers of his right hand through one of the tight, square wire openings. That was what passed for a prematch handshake. On those fall afternoons seventeen years ago, excitement and confidence jumped through his fingers like electricity through a Long Island Lighting Company power line.

Remembrances of those three-fingered "handshakes" surfaced last year, when the fatherhood fraternity initiated me on the birth of my first child, Veronica. I am now learning that the lessons my father taught me about *being there* are not always so easy to apply.

I work out of my home in Arlington, Virginia, as a free-lance journalist. My wife Margie, who left a good job with the Norfolk-Southern Railroad Company when she became a mom, is at home caring for our daughter. Like everyone else, I am trying to get ahead. But at numerous times during the day, I drop what I am doing and skip downstairs from my second-floor office to help out or just to play. Veronica is a magnet. I am beginning to realize what drew my father to those high school tennis matches of mine.

When my mother became pregnant with my brother early in 1951, the year after I was born, Dad was working for Delmar Construction Company on a job at Bruckner Boulevard in the Bronx. He told his boss that he was taking two weeks of paternity leave when the baby was born so that he could stay home and help out. Dad might as well have told him that Eisenhower was a Communist.

On a Sunday morning in early December, Mom went into labor. That night, Dad called his boss. He would not be in for two weeks, he said. By midweek, his boss was pleading with him to get up to Bruckner Boulevard. Dad finally agreed to go in for part of the second week, though he took part of the third week off as well.

Family also came between Dad and Lizza Brothers, another big New York construction company. Al Lizza wanted Dad, his chief engineer, to work Saturdays, which he did. But when those weekends began to pile up like railroad cars in a wreck, Dad objected. Weekends were for the family. Pretty soon, he was spending whole weeks with us while he looked for a new job.

When he spent time with my brother, sister, and me, Dad always participated fully in body and spirit. His was never an obligatory presence. When I was a boy, almost every dad took his sons to Madison Square Garden, Yankee Stadium, and, later, Shea Stadium to watch the New York professional sports teams. Few fathers, though, led their kids to the door of the home-team dressing room to gawk at their heroes as they filed out.

MICHAEL WEISBROT

Dad not only led us to Olympus, he also tried to get photographs of us and our gods. Once, he nearly became the object of a Sophoclean tragedy. In his enthusiasm, he popped a flashbulb in the face of Gump Worsley, the gruff New York Ranger hockey team goalie. The Gumper did not care about Dad's good intentions. Clearly annoyed, Gump took his goalie stick, an imposing wooden scythe, and whipped it against the cement wall just outside the dressing room. It narrowly missed Dad's head.

For me, these days, *being there* means keeping enough diapers stacked on the dictionaries in my second-floor office. Sometimes it seems inconvenient to help out with Veronica during my working

hours, but I find myself doing it anyway. Often, on my way upstairs at
8:00 a.m., I pass our bedroom and hear her gleeful chattering. Out of
the darkness, Margie's eyes catch mine. They say silently what her
voice quickly confirms. She has been up several times during the
night, feeding an avidly nursing baby, and can get some much-needed
sleep if I take Veronica.

So up we go to my aerie, me and my daughter. I anchor her red
Sassy seat onto the side of my desk. Work invariably beckons. And for
a while, as a madly teething Veronica gnaws on a corner of my
appointment book, progress is mine. But she eventually insists on my
full attention.

Not much work gets done during those hours. This worries me. It is
not always easy to sort out my priorities so that Veronica comes out
on top. Yet Dad always seemed relaxed and content at my high school
tennis matches. Work could not give him the satisfaction that I think
he got from seeing my forehands and backhands starting to zing deep
into my opponent's court.

He taught me the importance of *being there*. It is a lesson I have not
forgotten.

23

Remembering a Father Who Mothered

Karen Hill Anton

She was eighteen when they married, he was fifty. My brother was born in March 1944, I in April 1945, my sister in April 1946. My mother didn't make it. She disappeared when my sister was a few months old. (Was it for two weeks, a month? I never knew for exactly how long, but it was long enough for handbills to be passed out giving a description of what she was "last seen wearing.") When found, she was committed to a state mental hospital, diagnosed as having amnesia. Though I knew what that word meant, it wasn't until much later that I could understand how much my mother must have wanted to forget.

"Put them in foster homes or an orphanage," my father was urged. "A man, especially a man of your age, can't possibly raise three young children."

The grandson of a slave, my father certainly never expected that life would be easy. Born in Mississippi in 1893, he was one of many blacks who went north in the early years of this century not only in search of the "promised land" but also to escape the constant threat of the lyncher's noose.

Although he managed to get an education, even graduating from Hampton Institute, it was clear to me as a young child that he thought himself fortunate to have any job at all. When he could find employment, it was often as a presser in a cleaning shop. I lied and told my friends he was a tailor, because even at that age, I appreciated the perceived difference between a professional and a laborer.

The cleaning shops he worked in were often local ones (so he could "keep an eye on us" while he worked). We would sometimes stop by to wave at him through a tiny window or go in the steamy back of the shop, knowing that no matter how busy he was, he would be glad to see us. The sweat poured off him as he stood over the large presser in the sleeveless undershirt he always worked in. "Daddy, can we have a nickel for a cream soda?" we'd ask.

The first word I knew how to spell was *Mississippi*—forward, backward, and fast. My father's education did not get him a job, but he passed on what he knew to his children. Gathering not only us but the neighbors' kids as well, he taught us our "sums," penmanship, and spelling. He knew American history thoroughly, especially that of the Civil War and the period of Reconstruction. "Please, Mr. Hill, tell us about the time..." sounded the pleas of the children as he told tales of the old South; and if he told a ghost story, you really got scared!

I knew my father had the only typewriter in the neighborhood—an old, heavy, black Royal—and probably the only set of encyclopedias. He was openly looked on as a resource and was often called on to draw up a petition, write a eulogy, chair the PTA or the community league, or lead a rent strike. When he wrote in his "fine hand," you could hear his pen scratching across vellum and bond; you could hear the pauses when he dipped the point into blue-black ink. His personal letters were treasures of wit, wisdom, and penmanship. The typed ones, to editors and congressmen, were fiery expressions of right and responsibility.

My oldest memory of anything is of my father coming back from work one day, and me running down our long hall (how long was that hall, I wonder now?) to meet him. He hunched down to half his size to give me a kiss and a hug, and I could see the top of his head and smell the pomade on his slicked-back hair. I must have been about four.

I remember, too, the time I accidentally ate the "dead man's meat," or gills of a crab. All of my friends said it would kill me, and I accepted their word, because we all knew that you *never* were supposed to eat *that part*. I was afraid to sleep that night, knowing death would claim me as soon as I closed my eyes. But then I realized that if I slept with Daddy I couldn't possibly die. So I crept into his bed and fell asleep with my head nestled on his chest and in the soft hair of his underarm. Surely death could not snatch me from the safety of my father— and it didn't.

"He does everything a woman would do for those kids."

Didn't he do everything a man would do? In any case, he accepted the challenge and responsibility of raising his children; he did what had to be done. So, of course, it never occurred to me that a man

MICHAEL WEISBROT

couldn't do what I'd seen my father do daily. Although the women's movement informed me that most men didn't do those things, I certainly knew they could. Friends joked that my husband would have a "hard act to follow."

When I was growing up, we didn't have a washing machine. I don't think anyone in our neighborhood had one. My father spent Saturday mornings scrubbing on a washboard in the bathtub with a large bar of brown laundry soap. I would trail after him as he took the enameled basin filled with well-wrung-out clothes and a paper bag of wooden clothespins up to the clothesline on the roof. Even after laundromats came into use, it took John Hill a long time to accept them.

All clothes were cotton then (remember?), and my father spent his Saturday nights ironing our dresses and pinafores with their wide sashes. ("Oh, he ties those girls' sashes as well as any woman.") At that time, no one even considered letting his or her hair go its own natural way, so he would spend hours straightening, braiding, and curling our hair so we could look "just as nice as the other little girls"—the girls who had mothers.

He could really "put the pots on," as I loved to brag to my friends, and make tasty soups and stews from just the bare essentials. He never had a cookbook; he never looked at a recipe; we didn't even have a measuring cup and spoons. We never ate canned or frozen anything. Sometimes our cupboard was truly bare, and there was "nothing in the icebox," but when I was a child I assumed everyone was hungry some of the time and that they were as happy as we were on the days when Daddy came home with heavy shopping bags.

Years later, when I was pregnant with my first child in Spain, I so longed for my father's cooking that I drew up lists of the things he made that I loved in an effort (not an entirely futile one, either) to assuage my cravings: stuffing for turkey, okra gumbo, black-eyed peas and rice, corn bread, biscuits, collard greens, mustard greens, baked beans. Later, when I wrote from Denmark of Nanao's birth, he promptly answered, "Now, Karen, you must begin to cultivate patience," and I wondered, how did he know? Nursing her, I found myself singing a song my father had sung to us at bedtime when we were very little. I hadn't heard that song for twenty years, and I'd never heard anyone other than my father sing it, but it seemed to be waiting in my throat for my baby.

Nothing was easy about not having a mother. It wasn't easy having to tell my father when I began menstruating or having to ask for the money to buy my first bra. It used to hurt like hell when some well-meaning person would say, "Your father is a wonderful and exceptional man," because it underscored the fact that we had no mother. I didn't like to be told that I, much more than my sister and brother, looked like and had the temperament of my father. But now there is pride in all that, and gratitude.

24

THE FATHER WITHIN

Bruce Bassoff

I have spent much of my adult life writing scholarly books and articles that my father says should be translated into English. Actually, academic discourse is not the kind of writing that was predicted of me as a child. "Sensitive" and "imaginative" were the terms most adults used, and my kindergarten teacher expected that I would become a "creative" writer. Although I wrote poems and short stories up through high school, that activity dried up in college. Throughout my ensuing career as a professor, I had ideas for creative work, but I felt stymied, unsure that I could bring those to fruition. Then, two years ago, I began writing a play. Not only was it eventually produced, but I went on to write five more plays and a children's novel.

Why the sudden burst of creativity? It has to do with accepting my father, with accepting my identification with him, and with accepting myself as a father. The force that released my creativity was my discovery of the father within.

The Father I Knew
Throughout much of my life, I dismissed my father's positive influence on me. Although I loved him and knew that he loved me, I resented his inability to become meaningfully involved in my life. He did not encourage me to talk to him, to confide in him; he did not make an effort to teach me things, to help me feel competent; and he did not encourage me to see him at his most competent—in the courtroom, for instance, where he worked as a trial lawyer.

By and large, I saw my father at home, where my mother dominated the scene. Although he sometimes resented my mother's bossiness, he also encouraged it with his passivity; and when he wanted to get back at her, he used passive-aggressive techniques, such as buying the wrong item at the store, or messing up some job around the house. I regarded him as an awkward bungler who often incurred my mother's wrath and frustration. I resented him for not being powerful.

This situation, not unusual in that generation of fathers, was compounded by my parents' physical disabilities. My mother had polio before she was two and has spent her entire life on crutches; my father also had polio and has one atrophied leg. But whereas my mother's disability elicited feelings of exaggerated loyalty, my father's brought forth feelings of resentment. Unable to compete with me physically and unwilling to challenge and guide me in other ways, he inspired my own sense of ineptness.

As I was to learn later, *my* father's inadequacies to some extent repeated *his* father's inadequacies. My father's parents, immigrants from Poland, were poor and tragically mismatched. Embittered by her life with my grandfather, my grandmother lived through her children. She ruled them with an iron hand and eventually turned them against their father, who did not express affection or even communicate with them. The good news is that this man became a wonderful grandfather—affectionate and humorous with all of his grandchildren.

Although my parents' marriage was much more loving, it had strains of its own that weakened my father's position. His manners and social behaviors, for example, bore traces of his early poverty. When he ate, he wolfed down his food as though afraid it would be taken away from him; he was uncultured and sometimes ill-mannered; in social situations, he often covered up his awkwardness with inappropriate bursts of aggression; and he assumed that anyone engaging in even a trivial business transaction was trying to cheat him. My mother, whose upbringing was much more refined, was often put off by his tastes, manners, and emotional inadequacies. As I grew up, I became the male she wanted—"sensitive" and "intellectual." Even as a young child, I was convinced that she preferred me to my father.

My mother dominated the household, with my father's tacit approval. Because she made all the arrangements concerning my everyday affairs, because she was involved in my schooling, and because she encouraged me to confide in her, she was the linchpin of my life. But she was also my keeper. Once, when I was delirious with fever, I fantasized that I was a horse trying to win a race, but my mother was holding me back. Another time, frustrated by my sense of inhibition, I ran away from home. I dashed out the door of our apartment, down six flights of stairs, and over to Riverside Park, where I wandered until cold and fatigue drove me back home. Reentering our apartment house, I hid under the staircase, where I intended to spend the night; but my father came down to get me. Dragged into the elevator and then into the apartment to face my aggrieved mother, I resented the fact that he was acting as her agent and that he never indicated, by word or expression, that he admired my pluck.

My mother was the one I could count on to understand my feelings and to go to bat for me when necessary, but her alacrity proved debilitating. Once, my sixth-grade teacher asked all the boys to make model airplanes. Like my father, I was never very good with my hands, and I dreaded having to do the project. When I expressed my dread to my mother, she came to school and asked my teacher if it was really necessary for me to make a model airplane. After all, I was an intellectual—brilliant, in fact. Why did I have to make an airplane? For over thirty years, I have regretted the fact that my father did not step in and say, "Sylvia, let me handle this. Bruce, you've got to do the project. It doesn't matter whether or not your plane turns out as good as someone else's. What matters is that you try your best. In fact, I'll help you."

In need of a strong male figure to emulate, I searched elsewhere. When I was nineteen, my mother's father died and left me a sum of money that enabled me to go to Europe for the first time. In Paris I bought a motor scooter, which became my means of transportation around Europe. One day, having gone over the Alps on my Lambretta, I was headed toward Innsbruck in western Austria. As I motored through some fields, I saw an old man who resembled my grandfather—the same robust build. I called out to him questioningly, "Innsbruck?" "*Jawohl!*" he replied, leaning on his hoe and waving me ahead. The old man's hearty response and encouraging gesture have remained with me, a symbol of the man who points out the way to his son and encourages him to take it.

I entered adulthood longing to find this man—looking for him in teachers, in political leaders, and in therapists. What finally released me to write creatively was finding this figure in myself: in the father whom I had internalized without knowing it, and in the father that I myself had become.

MICHAEL WEISBROT

The Father I Discovered

In psychotherapy at the age of forty-four, I discovered positive tendencies in my relationship with my father. When I was nine, for example, he and I met my mother and some of their friends at a downtown movie theater. As we approached the theater, I noticed with dismay some stills of ballet dancers and the title *The Red Shoes* on the marquee. "Nothing doing," said a voice inside me, and I adamantly protested the choice of film. "Sylvia," said my father, "the boy doesn't want to see it. I'll take him to something else. You all enjoy yourselves." As we walked away, I could sense his relief, and I knew that he did not want to see *The Red Shoes* any more than I did. Playing hooky from my mother's cultural refinement, the two of us went to see *An Evening of Silent Film Comedies*. Charlie Chaplin, Buster Keaton, and Harold Lloyd had us roaring at the slapstick humor that my mother never enjoyed.

At other times, my father and I shared ritualized ways of escaping my mother's influence. On Tuesday nights, he and I would watch Milton Berle's comedy show—slapstick at its most vulgar and silly. Whenever my mother and sister joined us, their puzzlement and disapproval only added to the hilarity. My mother, to her credit, did little to discourage us. In one scene, when Milton Berle told his girlfriend that they should "make up" and a little man ran out yelling, "*Makeup!!!*" and smacked Uncle Miltie in the face with a large powder puff, my father and I roared hysterically while my mother, stone faced, turned to my sister and asked, "Do you think that's funny, Paula?" On other nights, my father and I would decline the classical music that my mother loved and instead fill the house with jazz, blues, and Puerto Rican music—the sounds that *he* loved. To this day, my tastes in music are eclectic.

In short, although my mother's intellectualism and refinement clearly guided my way, in the past few years I have come to understand the importance of my father's humor and vitality. Internalized, these traits have supported me through periods of enormous pain and depression, and they have opened pathways to the more expressive parts of myself. As a father, I now share these qualities with my children, who enjoy my spontaneity more than my intellectualism.

I have also come to value my father's determination. Often clumsy and inept at home, this "bull in a china shop" was apparently persevering and accomplished in many other aspects of his life. Although I never saw his doggedness at work in the courtroom, I did know that he had worked his way through law school by selling newspapers and that the landlord-tenant work he did demanded tenacity. And I admired the way he pursued new skills later in life: the way he learned to swim in his sixties; the way he practiced calligraphy; the way he studied French phrases while visiting France with my mother, my wife, and me; and the way he took up acting after retiring from law.

Very recently, he shared a story he had never told before. Teased by some of his schoolmates because of the brace he wore on his leg, he threw off the brace and challenged one of his tormentors. I pride myself on this same sort of determination. And I got it, I am sure, from my father.

The Father I Became

My attitude toward my father became more self-conscious when I became a father. With the birth of my first child, Leah, I made a conscious decision to be an involved parent in ways that my father and my father's father had not been. In fact, my worst outbursts of temper have accompanied those rare moments of feeling that my wife was excluding me from the dyad she formed with my daughter.

One New Year's Eve, in the throes of feeling rejected from their cozy "nest," I stormed out of the house and went to a double feature at a nearby movie theater. Influenced both by my violent reaction and by her own sensitivity and goodwill, my wife seldom excluded me again.

Fathering was definitely becoming the priority I wanted it to be. For one thing, because my job as a college professor allowed me considerable flexibility, I was able to see my daughter several times a day as well as at night. In addition, my wife and I established a weekly "family day"—a day reserved for walking and doing other things as a threesome.

When my son came along three years later, my urge to be close to him manifested immediately in a tendency to snatch him out of bed, throw him over my shoulder, stuff a diaper in my back pocket, and take him for long walks around town. As Jonathan got older, I delighted in doing things with him that my father had not been able to do with me. Out in the yard, we played "pop-ups." I would toss a tennis ball high in the air, and he would circle under it and try to catch it. Sometimes it would land yards away; other times it would bounce off some part of his body. Once in a while, he would catch it. The more we played and the older he got, the more often he caught the pop-ups.

As the years passed, it was fascinating to watch certain differences unfold in my relationships with each child. With my daughter, I shared my imagination. We would take long walks together, and I would make up stories about anything that caught her attention: flowers, berries, trees, animals. To this day, we share an interest in theater. In fact, my first play was inspired by Leah and her fellow thespians.

With my son, I shared my aggressive energy and physical competence. When he was very young, we constantly rolled over the floor together, enjoying the movement and the struggle. As he grew older, we took to roughhousing in ways that sometimes annoyed his mother and sister. We wrestled, we prodded and poked each other, and we pushed each other around. Even now that he is fifteen, we rough-and-tumble on occasion, just to remind ourselves of our mutual affection and identity as aggressive males. We also played baseball, basketball, and football together. I took pride in teaching him everything I knew, and the competence he demonstrated reassured me, whenever I doubted my worth as a father, that I had given him *something*.

Such doubts were more pronounced with my son than with my daughter. With her, I always felt confident that I was being a good father and that she was growing up strong and happy. With my son, who seemed to have a preternatural sensitivity to my moods and spiritual travails, I was less certain of my positive influence. Sometimes, I wondered if my unresolved frustrations and insecurities might be undermining his sense of security. Nevertheless, my determination to be a strong father for him fueled my inner sources of strength and vitality.

In autumn 1988, my first play was produced, and my children's novel was accepted for publication. The play was dedicated to my wife and daughter; the novel, to my son. My daughter played one of the roles in the production, and my father, who has been acting in plays for senior citizens and occasionally writing them as well, flew out from New York for opening night. As he proffered some roses to Leah while she was taking her bow, I loved him more fully and unequivocally than ever before. It became strikingly clear that, within the scope of his life experience, he had been as encouraging as he could be and that he would not begrudge me for having gone further.

PART VI:
THE FUN OF FATHERING

25

A New Father's Field Guide

Bruce Leigh

So you want to be a father. That's a worthy ambition—perhaps the ultimate creative pursuit. But be advised, real-life fathering is no stroll in the garden. You'll be in unknown territory: no maps, no easy compass headings. You'll be tested and pushed to your limits, dealing day to day with a strange little creature called a baby. There will be questions, lots of them, and not much in the way of answers—until now. *A New Father's Field Guide* just may be your ticket out of the wilderness into the light of unrestrained, inventive, and totally successful fathering.

I. Handling the Rest of the World

The Postpartum Identity Crisis

The early stages of new fatherhood will most likely fragment your personality and leave you straddling the abyss between two separate realms; they may possibly turn you schizoid. New fathers are easily recognized on the street: they often talk to themselves, smile and laugh without provocation, or walk into things. They are almost always carrying something.

To the extent that you have become immersed in the mystery of your new family, you will find that you have also become estranged from the world outside. The mail continues to arrive, the phone rings, people speak to you (usually in your language), but in everything there is a sense of unreality. People who know you may claim not to know you anymore. Your life outside the family unit will seem in turn absurd, dull, repulsive, or simply illusory. Your actions will appear dreamlike. You may be surprised to observe yourself doing such things as working, riding subways, or polishing your shoes. There will be no sense to any of this. Logic will have flown out the window, leaving you, from time to time, worried.

The best way to handle all this is to stop going out. When you must occasionally face the outside world, try not to think of yourself as some deranged, pathological type who had found fatherhood too much of a strain. Actually, the more distorted and uninteresting the outside world appears to you, the more capable you are of fathering. There is really no choice: If you are going to give yourself totally to your baby's first year, to give him the kind of fathering he needs and deserves, you must get used to the idea of life not being the same anymore.

Jobs

Most people will tell you that having a job is a good thing, especially if you are a new father. Jobs give off money, and babies are expensive items. However, jobs also consume time. It's a fact that the more you work, the less able you will be to father, but the better able you will be to pay the bills. That, in a nutshell, is the dilemma.

If you are enormously wealthy, this dilemma doesn't exist. If you are simply rich and also have a job, just announce that you are taking a one-year leave of absence. If you don't have money but possess daring and a strong faith in benevolent destiny, do the same thing. You will probably be fired immediately, which will at least provide a few unemployment checks.

If none of these approaches appeal to you, use your imagination. One possibility is to apply for a grant. Fathering grants per se do not exist, but that doesn't mean you shouldn't start the ball rolling. All it takes is a clever proposal.

Make up a good story, such as, you've decided to take your wife and newborn to Antarctica for a year to study the effects of extreme climate on mother and infant development. Tally up your estimated expenses and send it in. You might just be surprised to receive a fat check in the mail, along with an application for the CIA.

Friends

A real friend is someone who doesn't mind being ignored for a year. This may sound harsh, but your world is built on new priorities now.

Friends are people to whom you can tell the truth. "I'm not the same guy I was," you tell them. "I've changed. I mean, something has come over me."

"You're not changed," they say. "You just have a kid now, that's all."

Those who have kids will simply leave you alone. There will be areas of dead space between you and the others; your orbits will no longer intersect. It's not their fault. Not having children, they can't be expected to understand.

You will become to them an object of awe, an enigma, a hopeless case. They will try to lure you into the same old activities: a night slumped over a bar, a game of squash, or a double-date at the movies. "Bring the kid along," they will say. "No one will mind!"

To one degree or another, your new fatherhood will be controversial. Friends may whine on the phone, claim rejection, or send you letters filled with subtle accusations.

The best thing to do is to settle this issue early. You have to determine which friends can accommodate the new you, the father, and which ones can't. A simple questionnaire will suffice, an example of which is available below:

1. Would you shake hands with me if you knew with almost total certainty that my hand had traces of fresh baby poo on it?
2. How would you react if my baby spit up on your new suit? On your beige rug? On your new girlfriend's dress?
3. When you think of babies, you think primarily of:
   a. pets
   b. small humans requiring vast amounts of time and love
   c. someone with no marketable skills
   d. an unfortunate state of being to be avoided at all costs
4. If you discovered you were about to become a father, you would:
   a. figure out who you could blame
   b. send out job applications overseas
   c. break into song
   d. contemplate suicide

Relatives

Relatives, especially those in the immediate family, are like homing pigeons when it comes to babies.

If there are relatives within two thousand miles of you and they are left to their own devices, you can expect them to show up anywhere from an hour to three days after the baby is born. As a new father with a new family, you may feel under siege. Your wife won't be of too much help. She will say things like, "Just don't answer the door," or,

JOHN SCHOENWALTER

"Leave a note on the mailbox." You will quickly realize the responsibility for coping with all the relatives is yours.

First, you can try telling them you'd like to be alone for a while. They will think this odd, but if you insist, they will offer to stay with your wife and baby while you go off by yourself. You will then explain you mean the three of you: daddy, mommy, and baby. This news will be greeted with tense silence. Finally, you will be asked how long you intend to hibernate.

"Not long," you will answer. "Three or four years at the most. Just long enough to get settled." Laugh after saying this. (You mean it, of course, but you must always laugh anyway. They are, after all, your parents, or hers. If it weren't for them, there wouldn't be you, etc.). Tell them to come back in two weeks or so.

Eventually, however, all stalling techniques fail. They descend upon you: parents, grandparents, in-laws, siblings, even aunts you've never met before.

How to survive:

1. Be suspicious of relatives who preface their remarks with "I don't believe in telling new parents how to raise their kids, but . . ."

2. If questioned about your plans for raising the child, be vague. Say something like. "Well, we'll just have to see how it goes." Don't say, "We are going to leave that up to the baby." If you carelessly say something like this, laugh. Laugh a lot. The relatives will assume you are under some form of new parent's stress and be conciliatory.

3. If you get completely fed up, reverse your tactics. Start acting crazy. Say, "We don't believe in polyester pajamas," and, "We've decided to let the baby sleep in our bed." Likewise, "We thought we wouldn't use any diapers, just clean it up when we come across it."

Someone may take you aside and suggest you get a grip on yourself. Another may slip you some cash. All will look concerned. Finally, they will ignore you entirely, concentrating on the baby.

As disagreeable as this might be to the baby, he probably won't remember it. You can always make it up to him later on.

II. Is There Sex after Birth?

This is a touchy subject, but one no new father can neglect facing indefinitely. Statistically, it has been proven that most new fathers think about sex less after their babies are born. This is OK for a while, because most new mothers think about sex almost not at all. After a while, though, desire begins to creep back, usually surfacing at the least opportune time.

If you are actively fathering, and your significant other is actively mothering, there are two factors to consider: energy and time. Fathering consumes vast numbers of calories. A happy, active father has no sense of time passing. Furthermore, you may think about sex for days before anything can be done about it. Your wife gives you the "I want it, I need it" look every chance she gets, but the two of you just can't seem to get together. You may begin to feel frustrated; you are, after all, a man as well as a father. What to do?

By now you will have realized that nothing about life can be thought of in the same terms as before the baby arrived on the scene. Sex is different. Here are a few things to bear in mind that will help make sex possible:

1. Be imaginative (this goes without saying) in all areas: subtle sex games, surreptitious tactile stimulations, odd locations and positions.

2. Be ready at a minute's notice—no extensive warm-ups, no over-indulgence in foreplay. You must be prepared when the moment strikes.
3. Play music and kiss a lot to muffle lovemaking sounds. Bondage ideas might work well here.
4. Don't do it too close to the crib, unless of course baby is in the living room amusing himself quietly. Even if you're not loud, most babies pick up on the kind of energy we're talking about. A sleeping baby will almost certainly wake up if his parents are having sex nearby.
5. Since you never want to leave your baby alone out of view, try the following: Wait for your baby to have a quiet, self-contained moment by himself. Undress quickly and have sex standing up, with just your two heads discreetly peering around a corner or doorway to maintain visual contact. Smile and talk softly whenever he looks at you, but don't overdo it. If you chatter too enticingly he'll know something is up and come right over. Don't be disconcerted if he turns toward you and laughs. He probably knows what's happening and thinks the two of you are hilarious.
6. If nothing seems to be working, consider a little excursion to Grandma's. After depositing the baby on Grandma's lap and while Grandpa chatters away in baby-talk, the two of you can casually disappear into the bathroom. You'll be surprised at how much you can accomplish before somebody notices you are missing.

III. A Word on Baby Sounds

Many people, including several experts, will dispute that the *Da* sound is baby's first real utterance and claim the *Ma* sound as primary and supreme.

True, many babies may *Ma* before they *Da*, but there is an inherent distinction that renders the comparison irrelevant. A baby *Ma*'s in the same way that he coos or gurgles, as a spontaneous expression of himself. As far as baby can tell, he is not separate from mommy; the two of them are extensions of the same being.

The *Da* sound, on the other hand, is an active assertion of the "other": father, friend, guide, separate and intimate object.

Once your baby *Da*'s for the first time, there will be no stopping him. *Da* will become central to his vocal universe, the syllable upon which he will build his entire first-year sound system.

A List of Early Sounds Based on the Da Principle

Da: The original impulse, referring to you, Da, and to every other object of interest in the world.

Dada: The multiplication of one *Da* into two. (No cause for alarm in you.) Also, a twentieth-century art form that takes its name from the tendency babies have to reduce by force anything in their path to a single and profound *Da*.

Ga/Nga: Probably of African origin. A name for the primordial *Da*.

Hida/Heyda: Usually combined in various ways to form rhythmic chants, or little songs about Da.

Bla: Often blurted out spontaneously, with a protruding tongue. Studies show links to the *Da* which are as yet unspecified.

Blablabla: Clearly a call for a *Bla* response from Da.

Ba: A simple *Da* offshoot, usually spoken on the in-breath.

Eeeeya/Eeeya Da: This comes a bit later and works well with pointing fingers. A possible variation is **Whodat Da**. When put in the interrogative, this may mean, "Who is that, Da?"

Eeeeow Da: Possibly a call for Da to meow.

Wawawa: A primitive chant, frequently employed while examining incomprehensible objects, such as dust balls, snowstorms, and fashion magazines. *Da* may appear as punctuation.

It is, of course, important for babies to hear the language they will eventually be asked to speak. Talk to your baby a lot, whether it is in English, Swahili, or Serbo-Croatian. At the same time, don't forget to speak his own language with him. He isn't locked into your narrative style, so don't try too hard to translate. The vital thing is your participation. He needs to feel he can communicate with you, Da.

In addition to making sounds, your baby will use a nonverbal grammar to get across to you. This may include clapping, waving, blinking, pointing, head shaking, and nodding. There are also the animal sounds the two of you have practiced. Try to work all this material into your conversations. Variety and timing are important. For instance, if he points, you growl. If he blinks, you blink back and head shake. If he nods, you clap. When he claps, you bark. Got the idea?

Hypothetical Conversation between Baby and Father

BABY: *Hida Hey Dada.*
FATHER: (deep voice) *Da Daaaa.*

BABY: ("baboon growl") *Eeeeeeeeeeya Da* (finger pointing recklessly).

FATHER: *Eeeeeeeeee Eeeeeeya Ya* (which slips into "parrot sound" finished with a conventional "bird tweet").

BABY: (shrieks and lunges) *Hidadada* (pointing finger this time up father's nose).

FATHER: *Eeeeooooowwwwwwwww* (then "dog growl," easing into a few high barks).

BABY: *Wa Wa Nga Da* (both hands slap father's head).

FATHER: (points and grunts) *Oooooooh Aah Eeeee*.

BABY: *Bababa Da*.

FATHER: *Bla Bla*.

BABY: (high-pitched scream into father's ear, pointing finger into eye) *Da Da Ga*.

FATHER: (lapsing into English) *I Am Da Da*.

BABY: (shaking head and laughing) *Da*.

26

The Fun of Fathering

Patch Adams

The lap: that wide playground space along the body's front. The lap represents a very special place in fathering, because it is the first place most dads play with their kids. Here is where the deepest roots of love are made. O lap, o place of holy tryst, do we ever stare at other things the way we do at our kids in our lap? You, the parent, gaze transfixed into a vortex of beauty that you feel you had some hand in creating. This may be nature's greatest gift to humans, the participation in a miracle.

Touching, rubbing, and caressing all develop in the lap. For weeks after they were born, I held my kids in my lap—mostly sleeping but always with radiant hope in their faces. Hey, that's fun! And when the tiny wiggly things awake, all eyes and ears, they know you are you, and they totally trust you. Fun? Whew! These are the basic day-to-day foundations for the fun of fathering: the meat-and-potatoes stuff. But the deepest fun lies in the germinating love between father and son. (I might as well digress here and say that I have a thirteen-year-old son, Atomic Zagnut, and a two-year-old son, Lars Zig. I have no daughters. I know I would interact differently with daughters, because I've played with many girl kids and lived with several in my group house.) This all starts in the lap: bouncing, sleeping, sitting, climbing (one of my favorites, as I get to impersonate an animated jungle gym), hanging, resting, diaper-changing, and, all this time, touching. In holding is delight. For years, kids crave being on your lap.

Hand in hand with the fun of touching is the fun of exploration. The lap is always there, secure acreage, so eventually kids branch off to explore the world. Over the years the exploring only gets more complex. There is terrific fun in exploring my interests with my boys, but equally tickling has been Zag's introducing his interests to me.

You see, I was and am a nerd, preoccupied with science labs and books. But early on, Zag chose to do sports, and if I wanted time with him, I had to participate in sports. Football, basketball, and baseball sessions came and went with the seasons: not just street play, but regular twice-weekly games. As Zag began competitive sports at a very young age, I have had the privilege of watching numerous hilarious athletic misadventures, such as basketball games won on scores of 4-2.

Another recurring joy Zag has given me is our annual fishing trip with "the boys." Nine years ago, he said he wanted to go fishing. Not having any experience in this field, I called some fishing friends who live in cabins they've built in rural Virginia. Mind you, these are rugged country men. For nine years in a row now we've gone, stayed at the cabins, fished all day, and played the traditional poker game at night: seven card, high-low, quarter ante. We stay up late, talk about how much we love our wives, and tell dirty jokes. We look forward to the time when Lars is four, so he can join us.

At times our father-son explorations have blatant educational qualities, which I suspect are expanding as we grow older. I really enjoyed teaching Zag to juggle (he's now better than me) and rope walk. I am thrilled now to be able to shoot pool with him on a weekly basis. It's a time for adult talk over my favorite game. We're forming lifetime rituals.

I am passionate about silliness, and my sons have enhanced that in me from the beginning. My memory yields the following moments, precious gems collected to keep me warm: the torrential rain in the suburbs, when we stripped to underwear and lay in the gutters. The time on the London train, when Zag surprised my wife, Lynda, and me by tying our shoes together under the table. My fortieth birthday party, when Zag pied me in the face and was, in turn, pied by another kid. The stink bomb I broke in the van on the way camping, to great squeals of delight from Zag, four of his friends, and my clownish friend Dave. The time two years ago when we oozed together in a mud pit we made with friends. (I told you sons are different from daughters.) There is a strong practical joker ethic in our house which can backfire on the beginner. I wear clownish pants with elastic waistbands, and Dave will often deftly pull them down, leaving me standing in my colorful underwear. Well, Zag wanted in on the fun, so once, at a formal reception, he did the same thing—only with less success in keeping the underwear in place.

JILL FINEBERG

On another note, I'd like to put in a plug here for the fun of discipline. Child-rearing is, by far, the most complex, taxing task in life. I didn't know I had anger and frustration in such quantities until I became a father. Children can push one to one's limits, and sometimes in a very short time. At first this realization is incredibly disconcerting, embarrassing, and foundation-shattering, but I have a keen interest in primatology, and that has helped me cope. It seems to me that a father's role is to help define and enforce limits. The male gorilla is mostly involved in child-rearing by his presence. He "displays" when the kids get out of hand. I, too, can feel the silver hairs bristle on my back when my sons act in a way unbefitting meaningful community life. I do not delight in the anger itself, but appreciate the mechanisms nature has given us to care for every need in child-rearing. The natural role of the mother is so obvious and ancient that it's nice to feel deep roots for the role of the dad as well.

This leads me to the fun of family—not just the immediate one but the community family as well. Yes, a holy part of fathering is the inter-play of dad, mom, and the kids. There is an intoxicating potential here to feel unity. Children can strengthen the bonds that hold their parents together by reflecting the love that a man and a woman have for each other. Each parent brings to the relationship his or her individuality. Their child is a true mixture, both genetic and behavioral, of both of them.

It is through my children that I feel linked to the whole evolution-ary process, feel a part of a line of life that has stretched 3,000 million years. My boys force me to feel a part of today and to have an interest in the future. Whomever you are (and in my case, however odd), when others see you as part of a happy family, much is forgiven and much trust is built, because the concept of family transcends all cul-tural differences. I feel that much of my personal freedom has been enhanced by my having a family. This means I can pursue levels of fun (particularly with other people, where most of my fun comes from) far beyond the limits of my individuality. This invested involvement with the future and other people helps keep my motivation alive to work for a better world, because I have personal contact with the inheritors.

The fun of fathering is at the very core of finding meaning in life. Seen selfishly, fathering is a touching marathon with perpetual play-mates. Cosmically, it offers a shortcut to feeling a part of the universe. I'm not speaking here of some rare precious commodity available only to a select few, but simply of the day-to-day life of a conscious, involved father. Play on!

27

My Baby Loves the Grateful Dead

Alan Reder

My baby loves the Grateful Dead. Loves them so much that the quickest cure at our place for an onset of persistent fussiness is rocking Ariel in her daddy's arms to "Touch of Gray," "China Cat Sunflower," "Bertha," or any other Grateful Dead tune of ancient or recent vintage.

And when baby won't go to sleep or (shudder!) wakes in the wee, wee hours of the night? Do I keep the lights down to the edge of the visible spectrum and walk baby back and forth, miles and miles in a crushingly dull, soundless void? Do I struggle heroically to outlast her, hoping she falls asleep on my shoulder before I fall asleep on my feet?

No way, José. We party. On goes the living room light. On goes the stereo. We pop in one of daddy's hundreds of live Dead tapes and dance, baby and daddy, swaying and stepping out to the syncopated beat and good vibrations. It works wonders. Baby's asleep three to four times faster than any conventionally wise method has yet yielded. Many rock critics find the Grateful Dead too "laid back," putting down their space-is-the-place music as "somnambulistic." I heartily disagree but must grudgingly admit that when it comes to my five-month-old daughter, my own flesh and blood, my argument suffers.

At first, my wife and I were prone to do the supposedly tried and true to quiet our daughter—you know, trudging around with her in an environment of dim light and white noise. We did it just the way the books said, often for hours on end. So when baby would finally buy a ticket to Dreamland, the skeptic in each of us couldn't help wondering if she would have just gone to sleep after that long of a span no matter what we did.

I, particularly, was miserable about the prospects of any more long nights without auditory or visual stimulation. I finally decided that if I was going to be up walking her for hours anyway, by God, I was going to try to enjoy myself. That meant music.

It took just one trial to see that I'd stumbled on a winner. In fact, the initial results, baby quieting and her muscles slackening, were obvious in the first few minutes. Victory—a deeply slumbering infant—was mine soon after. Still, I can't really take credit for any brilliant insight here. My method seemed so illogical and counterproductive on the face of it that I have only one defense for first trying it; I didn't know any better.

Now, though dozens of subsequent successes have confirmed the method's viability, I'm not about to rewrite the books on baby care. How could I? I've never read any. I do, however, have a theory about the happy accident of my success. Call it the Theory of Contagious Relaxation, which derives from my earlier Theory of Contagious Agitation. Remember the last time you lay in bed unable to sleep? Remember how you got increasingly uptight with each passing minute about your chances of getting at least some shut-eye before the alarm went off? Which uptightness, of course, only further sabotaged your efforts.

The self-sabotage works about the same way, I figure, when walking your baby. If you let her cries or the fact that it's 3:00 a.m. get to you, the resulting tension in your body can't help but affect that little body that you're holding so closely.

My solution: Use that principle to your advantage. Transmit relaxation. I put on music that relaxes me and that I wouldn't mind listening to all night, if it comes to that (though it never does). No resentment of the disturbance to my slumber, no anxiety about the duration of our living room trek. I'm just dancing with my little girl, and what could be better than that?

The choice of music has something to do with what works here, too. I don't always put on the Grateful Dead for us—the Bhundu Boys (a group from Zimbabwe), David Lindley and El Rayo X, and Bob Marley and the Wailers are also on our hit list. But I do always choose "body music," music that moves the body with its rhythms. Rhythms that are syncopated without being frenetic have a naturally relaxing effect on the body. Baby may not understand the lyrics she hears, but her muscles love that beat.

As for volume, I haven't seen that it matters. When I listen to

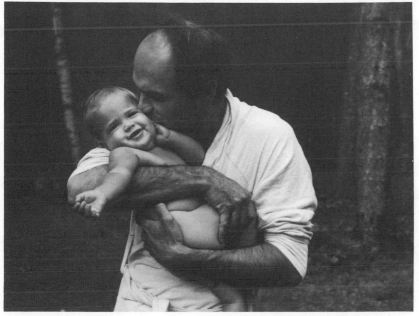

SUSAN LIRAKIS NICOLAY

electric music, I like the volume up where I can feel it. Certainly, I would never play music so loud that my baby's hearing was endangered, but we listen to our Grateful Dead at considerably more than lullaby level.

It probably didn't hurt that within four hours after Ariel's birth, I had her listening to the music that she now delights in. Psychological types might say I "conditioned" her, that I could just as easily have accustomed her to the "CBS Evening News."

But I prefer to think that the music itself does the work. Therefore, it ought to work for your baby, too. So try it. It might take fifteen minutes, or forty-five minutes, to get your baby to sleep this way. But that beats the heck out of the alternative, not only in time but also in entertainment value.

And by the way, only use music that *you* enjoy. That's a crucial part of the formula. But be forewarned. If ZZ Top or the "1812 Overture" don't get you the results Ariel and I get with our choices, try body music, something with a little wiggle in it, something that makes you and baby want to get up and shake your booties (the ones you share, not the ones baby wears).

CONTRIBUTORS

William Sears, M.D., is the father of seven. He is also assistant professor of pediatrics at the University of Southern California School of Medicine, author of seven books on child care, and a practicing pediatrician in San Clemente, California. His books are available in most bookstores or by mail order from Creative Parenting Resources, P.O. Box 7238, Capistrano Beach, CA 92624.

Jack R. Heinowitz, M.D., is a father, a psychologist, a marriage and family therapist, and the author of *Pregnant Fathers: How Fathers Can Enjoy and Share the Experiences of Pregnancy and Childbirth* (Prentice-Hall). He is co-director, with his wife, Ellen, of Parents As Partners Associates in San Diego. *Pregnant Fathers* and the pamphlet *Being Pregnant Together* are available through his office at 411 Thorn Street #E, San Diego, CA 92103, or by calling (619) 692-4038.

"Pregnant Fathers" first appeared as "The Pregnant Father" in *Mothering* 27, Spring 1983.

Ken Druck, author of *The Secrets Men Keep: Breaking the Silence Barrier* (Ballantine, 1987), is a clinical and consulting psychologist and speaker. He is in private practice in San Diego, California, and appears regularly on national radio and television. Ken and his wife Karen, also a therapist, live with their two daughters, Jenna and Stephanie, and with Kelsey, the son of their friend Terry, who is now deceased.

"Supporting the Supporting Father" first appeared in *Mothering* 43, Spring 1987.

Victor LaCerva, M.D., is a pediatrician working in public health and a child at heart. His passions include music making, aikido, and creating men's conferences. He lives and plays with his wife, Laura, and daughters, Gina and Rosa, in Tesuque, New Mexico.

"Dearest Papa" first appeared in *Mothering* 33, Fall 1984.

Robert Millar is a free-lance writer and instructor of music and humanities at Skyline Community College in northern California. He lives in Walnut Creek, California, with his wife and two sons.

"How Parenting Civilizes Us" first appeared in *Mothering* 36, Summer 1985.

Peter J. Dorsen, M.D., practiced internal medicine for eleven years and now devotes himself to free-lance writing, sports medicine, cross-country skiing, and his children, Bria, Gabriella, and Katarina. His wife, Susy, is a classical flutist and a tennis player. The family lives in Minneapolis, Minnesota, with two dogs and two cats.

"Fathering: A Matter of Enlightenment" was originally published in *Mothering* 51, Spring 1989.

John McMahon lives in Santa Fe, New Mexico.

"Growing Up with Your Kids" first appeared in *Mothering* 21, Fall 1981.

David Morton is a graphic artist and free-lance photographer living in Santa Fe, New Mexico.

"Early Days as a Stepfather" first appeared in *Mothering* 21, Fall 1981.

Paul Michaels is a free-lance writer who lives with his daughter, Heather, in northern California. They both love opera.

"The Litany of Childhood" first appeared in *Mothering* 33, Fall 1984.

Joseph Polselli is a magazine writer and novelist. His first novel, *Drums for a Different War*, was published in March 1984. Joseph, along with Jim and Randi, are home-schooling Mikaela (now age six) at their homestead in northern California.

"Being Baba" first appeared in *Mothering* 39, Spring 1986.

Don Richmond, a musician, lives in Alamosa, Colorado. He has two daughters, Heather and Laurel.

"Parable" first appeared in *Mothering* 2, Winter 1977.

Posy Gering tells stories especially for fathers—and mothers and kids. She lives in Seattle, Washington.

"Love, Father" first appeared in *Mothering* 27, Spring 1983.

John Byrne Barry is a writer and graphic designer for the Sierra Club in San Francisco. He lives with his wife, Laurie, and son, Sean, across the bay in Berkeley.

"Balancing Fatherhood and Career" first appeared in *Mothering* 51, Spring 1989.

Howard Skeffington is stationed at Ramstein Air Base, Germany, with the Air Force. He is a part-time writer, musician, and teacher. He and his wife, Peggy W. Skeffington, a La Leche League leader, are the parents of Jacob and Lael.

"Weathering the Storm Together" first appeared in *Mothering* 45, Fall 1987.

Charles Fletcher is the co-owner of NextStep Publications, a desktop media production and consulting business. He lives in Astoria, Oregon, with his wife, Jan, and their three children.

Randall Shultz, a refugee from the corporate world, owns and operates an advertising and public relations agency in Albuquerque, New Mexico. He is currently working on a book entitled *DaddyTrack: How to Spend More Time with Your Kids without Killing Your Career.*

Jack Maslow is a clinical social worker in private practice in Marin County, California. His clinical interests include work with divorced fathers and their relationships with their children. He also does parent-teen conflict mediation. Jack is remarried, and his son, Ari Michael Maslow, is now a college student. Their relationship remains close and loving.

"Noncustodial Fathers" first appeared in *Mothering* 46, Winter 1988.

Bruce Low is a California father and security consultant. His son, Uri, is six years old.

"Child Support That Really Is" first appeared in *Mothering* 42, Winter 1987.

William F. Van Wert teaches film and creative writing at Temple University. He is the author of two film books as well as two books of short stories, *Tales for Expectant Fathers* (New York: Dial Press, 1982) and *Missing in Action* (New York: York Press, 1990) and a novella *The Discovery of Chocolate* (Flagstaff: Word Beat Press, 1989). He is the father of three sons.

Sam Osherson, Ph.D., is a practicing psychotherapist and a teacher at Harvard University. Interested in the area of men's development, he is the author of *Holding On or Letting Go* (New York: The Free Press, 1980) and *Finding Our Fathers: How a Man's Life is Shaped by His Relationship with His Father* (New York: Ballantine, 1987). His wife, Julie, is a social worker. The Oshersons live with their children, Toby and Emily, in Cambridge, Massachusetts. *Finding Our Fathers* is now available as a Ballantine/Fawcett paperback ($8.95) at most book stores.

"Celebrate Father's Day" first appeared in *Mothering* 47, Spring 1988.

Steven Barlas is a free-lance journalist who lives in Arlington, Virginia, with his wife Margie Bell, a homemaker, and their two children.

"Lessons My Father Taught Me" first appeared in *Mothering* 30, Winter 1986.

Karen Hill Anton was born and raised in New York City. For the past fifteen years, she has lived with her husband, Bill Anton, a childhood friend, in Hamamatsu, Japan. Their four children are Nanao, Mie, Mario, and Lila. Karen writes regular columns for a Japanese language newspaper and *The Japan Times*. She is currently completing her first novel.

"Remembering a Father Who Mothered" first appeared in *Mothering* 35, Spring 1985.

Bruce Bassoff is professor of English at the University of Colorado, a produced playwright, and author of scholarly books and articles as well as of a children's novel, *Supercharged* (Bookmakers Guild, 1990). His wife Evelyn is a psychologist and the author of *Mothers and Daughters: Loving and Letting Go.* The Bassoffs live in Boulder, Colorado, with their children, Leah and Jonathan.

"The Father Within" first appeared in *Mothering* 54, Winter 1990.

Bruce Leigh is currently impersonating the regular humor columinist for *The Japan Times*. He, wife Michelle, and children Gabriel and Amber live in Sendai, Japan.

"Handling the Rest of the World" first appeared in *Mothering* 33, Fall 1984; "Is There Sex after Birth?" in *Mothering* 34, Winter 1985; and "A Word on Baby Sounds" in *Mothering* 35, Spring 1985.

Patch Adams is married to Lynda and father to two sons, Zag and Zig. He is a physician and director of the Gesundheit Institute, a model health care community in Arlington, Virginia. Members of the institute are currently building a free hospital that will carry no malpractice insurance and accept no third-party payments; they will live with their patients as friends. Patch has been a clown for thirty years.

Alan Reder writes on popular culture from his home in Encinitas, California. He wants readers to know that only in the way described is his daughter a Deadhead.

Other Books from John Muir Publications

Asia Through the Back Door, Rick Steves and John Gottberg (65-48-3) 336 pp. $15.95

Buddhist America: Centers, Retreats, Practices, Don Morreale (28-94-X) 400 pp. $12.95

Bus Touring: Charter Vacations, U.S.A., Stuart Warren with Douglas Bloch (28-95-8) 168 pp. $9.95

Catholic America: Self-Renewal Centers and Retreats, Patricia Christian-Meyer (65-20-3) 325 pp. $13.95

Complete Guide to Bed & Breakfasts, Inns & Guesthouses, Pamela Lanier (65-43-2) 512 pp. $15.95

Costa Rica: A Natural Destination, Ree Sheck (65-51-3) 280 pp. $15.95

Elderhostels: The Students' Choice, Mildred Hyman (65-28-9) 224 pp. $12.95

Europe 101: History & Art for the Traveler, Rick Steves and Gene Openshaw (28-78-8) 372 pp. $12.95

Europe Through the Back Door, Rick Steves (65-42-4) 432 pp. $16.95

Floating Vacations: River, Lake, and Ocean Adventures, Michael White (65-32-7) 256 pp. $17.95

Gypsying After 40: A Guide to Adventure and Self-Discovery, Bob Harris (28-71-0) 264 pp. $12.95

The Heart of Jerusalem, Arlynn Nellhaus (28-79-6) 312 pp. $12.95

Indian America: A Traveler's Companion, Eagle/Walking Turtle (65-29-7) 424 pp. $16.95

Mona Winks: Self-Guided Tours of Europe's Top Museums, Rick Steves (28-85-0) 450 pp. $14.95

The On and Off the Road Cookbook, Carl Franz (28-27-3) 272 pp. $8.50

The People's Guide to Mexico, Carl Franz (28-99-0) 608 pp. $15.95

The People's Guide to RV Camping in Mexico, Carl Franz with Steve Rogers (28-91-5) 256 pp. $13.95

Preconception: A Woman's Guide to Preparing for Pregnancy and Parenthood, Brenda Aikey-Keller (65-44-0) 236 pp. $14.95

Ranch Vacations: The Complete Guide to Guest and Resort, Fly-Fishing, and Cross-Country Skiing Ranches, Eugene Kilgore (65-30-0) 392 pp. $18.95

The Shopper's Guide to Mexico, Steve Rogers and Tina Rosa (28-90-7) 224 pp. $9.95

Ski Tech's Guide to Equipment, Skiwear, and Accessories, edited by Bill Tanler (65-45-9) 144 pp. $11.95

Ski Tech's Guide to Maintenance and Repair, edited by Bill Tanler (65-46-7) 144 pp. $11.95

A Traveler's Guide to Asian Culture, Kevin Chambers (65-14-9) 224 pp. $13.95

Traveler's Guide to Healing Centers and Retreats in North America, Martine Rudee and Jonathan Blease (65-15-7) 240 pp. $11.95

Undiscovered Islands of the Caribbean, Burl Willes (28-80-X) 216 pp. $12.95

22 Days Series
These pocket-size itineraries are a refreshing departure from ordinary guidebooks. Each author has an in-depth knowledge of the region covered and offers 22 tested daily itineraries through their favorite destinations. Included are not only "must see" attractions but also little-known villages and hidden "jewels" as well as valuable general information.

22 Days Around the World by R. Rapoport and B. Willes (65-31-9)
22 Days in Alaska by Pamela Lanier (28-68-0)
22 Days in the American Southwest by R. Harris (28-88-5)
22 Days in Asia by R. Rapoport and B. Willes (65-17-3)
22 Days in Australia by John Gottberg (65-40-8)
22 Days in California by Roger Rapoport (28-93-1)
22 Days in China by Gaylon Duke and Zenia Victor (28-72-9)

22 Days in Dixie by Richard Polese (65-18-1)
22 Days in Europe by Rick Steves (65-63-7)
22 Days in Florida by Richard Harris (65-27-0)
22 Days in France by Rick Steves (65-07-6)
22 Days in Germany, Austria & Switzerland by Rick Steves (65-39-4)
22 Days in Great Britain by Rick Steves (65-38-6)
22 Days in Hawaii by Arnold Schuchter (65-50-5)
22 Days in India by Anurag Mathur (28-87-7)
22 Days In Japan by David Old (28-73-7)
22 Days in Mexico by S. Rogers and T. Rosa (65-41-6)
22 Days in New England by Anne Wright (28-96-6)
22 Days in New Zealand by Arnold Schuchter (28-86-9)
22 Days in Norway, Denmark & Sweden by R. Steves (28-83-4)
22 Days In the Pacific Northwest by R. Harris (28-97-4)
22 Days in Spain & Portugal by Rick Steves (65-06-8)
22 Days In the West Indies by C. & S. Morreale (28-74-5)

All 22 Days titles are 128 to 152 pages and $7.95 each, except *22 Days Around the World* and *22 Days in Europe*, which are 192 pages and $9.95.

**"Kidding Around"
Travel Guides for Children**
Written for kids eight years of age and older. Generously illustrated in two colors with imaginative

characters and images. An adventure to read and a treasure to keep.

Kidding Around Atlanta, Anne Pedersen (65-35-1) 64 pp. $9.95
Kidding Around Boston, Helen Byers (65-36-X) 64 pp. $9.95
Kidding Around the Hawaiian Islands, Sarah Lovett (65-37-8) 64 pp. $9.95
Kidding Around London, Sarah Lovett (65-24-6) 64 pp. $9.95
Kidding Around Los Angeles, Judy Cash (65-34-3) 64 pp. $9.95
Kidding Around New York City, Sarah Lovett (65-33-5) 64 pp. $9.95
Kidding Around San Francisco, Rosemary Zibart (65-23-8) 64 pp. $9.95
Kidding Around Washington, D.C., Anne Pedersen (65-25-4) 64 pp. $9.95

Automotive Books

The Greaseless Guide to Car Care Confidence: Take the Terror Out of Talking to Your Mechanic, Mary Jackson (65-19-X) 224 pp. $14.95
How to Keep Your VW Alive (65-12-2) 424 pp. $19.95
How to Keep Your Subaru Alive (65-11-4) 480 pp. $19.95
How to Keep Your Toyota Pickup Alive (28-89-3) 392 pp. $19.95
How to Keep Your Datsun/ Nissan Alive (28-65-6) 544 pp. $19.95
Off-Road Emergency Repair & Survival, James Ristow (65-26-2) 160 pp. $9.95
Road & Track's Used Car Classics, edited by Peter Bohr (28-69-9) 272 pp. $12.95

Ordering Information
If you cannot find our books in your local bookstore, you can order directly from us. Your books will be sent to you via UPS (for U.S. destinations), and you will receive them approximately 10 days from the time that we receive your order. Include $2.75 for the first item ordered and $.50 for each additional item to cover shipping and handling costs. UPS will not deliver to a P.O. Box; please give us a street address. For airmail within the U.S., enclose $4.00 per book for shipping and handling. All foreign orders will be shipped surface rate; please enclose $3.00 for the first item and $1.00 for each additional item. Please inquire about foreign airmail rates.

Method of Payment
Your order may be paid by check, money order, or credit card. We cannot be responsible for cash sent through the mail. All payments must be made in U.S. dollars drawn on a U.S. bank. Canadian postal money orders in U.S. dollars are also acceptable. For VISA, MasterCard, or American Express orders, include your card number, expiration date, and your signature, or call (505)982-4078. Books ordered on American Express cards can be shipped only to the billing address of the cardholder. Sorry, no C.O.D.'s. Residents of sunny New Mexico, add 5.625% tax to the total.

Address all orders and inquiries to:
John Muir Publications
P.O. Box 613
Santa Fe, NM 87504
(505) 982-4078
(505) 988-1680 FAX